FLORIDA'S
CARNIVOROUS
PLANTS

Understanding, Identifying, and Cultivating
the State's Native Species

KENNY COOGAN

Pineapple Press
Palm Beach, Florida

Dedicated to
Ryan McGhee

Pineapple Press

An imprint of Globe Pequot, the trade division of
The Rowman & Littlefield Publishing Group, Inc.
4501 Forbes Blvd., Ste. 200
Lanham, MD 20706
www.rowman.com

Distributed by NATIONAL BOOK NETWORK

British Library Cataloguing in Publication Information available

Library of Congress Cataloging-in-Publication Data

Names: Coogan, Kenny, author.
Title: Florida's carnivorous plants : understanding, identifying, and cultivating the state's native species / Kenny Coogan
Description: Palm Beach, Florida : Pineapple Press, [2022] | Includes index and glossary.
Identifiers: LCCN 2021050331 (print) | LCCN 2021050332 (ebook) | ISBN 9781683342977 (paperback) | ISBN 9781683342960 (ebook)
Subjects: LCSH: Endemic plants—Florida. | Carnivorous plants—Florida. | Gardening—Florida. | Handbooks and manuals.
Classification: LCC SB432.7 .C66 2022 (print) | LCC SB432.7 (ebook) | DDC 35.09759—dc23/eng/20211028
LC record available at https://lccn.loc.gov/2021050331
LC ebook record available at https://lccn.loc.gov/2021050332

∞™ The paper used in this publication meets the minimum requirements of American National Standard for Information Sciences—Permanence of Paper for Printed Library Materials, ANSI/NISO Z39.48-1992.

Contents

FOREWORD   vi

PREFACE   vii

CARNIVOROUS PLANTS   1

CARNIVOROUS PLANT LIFE CYCLE   3

    Plant versus Animal Digestion   5

    Evolution   5

    Taxonomy   6

FLORIDA'S CARNIVOROUS PLANTS   11

    Draining the Swamp   13

    Women's Work   14

    Scientific Progress   17

    Ecosystems   18

GROWING CARNIVOROUS PLANTS   21

    Bogs and Containers   21

    Fertilizers   26

    Dormancy   26

    Light   27

    Pests   27

    Soil   28

    Water   28

    Carnivorous Plants as Insecticides   29

VENUS FLYTRAPS   31

NORTH AMERICAN PITCHER PLANTS   39

    Sarracenia alabamensis subsp. *wherryi*   43

    Sarracenia flava   44

    Sarracenia leucophylla   46

    Sarracenia minor   47

    Sarracenia psittacina   49

    Sarracenia rosea   50

    Sarracenia rubra subsp. *gulfensis*   53

BLADDERWORTS   57

    Utricularia amethystina   59

    Utricularia cornuta   60

    Utricularia floridana   60

    Utricularia foliosa   61

    Utricularia gibba   61

    Utricularia inflata   61

    Utricularia juncea   62

    Utricularia olivacea   62

Utricularia purpurea   62

Utricularia radiata   63

Utricularia resupinata   63

Utricularia simulans   63

Utricularia striata   64

Utricularia subulata   64

BUTTERWORTS   69

Pinguicula caerulea   71

Pinguicula ionantha   71

Pinguicula lutea   72

Pinguicula planifolia   73

Pinguicula primuliflora   74

Pinguicula pumila   75

SUNDEWS   77

Drosera brevifolia   78

Drosera capillaris   78

Drosera filiformis var. *floridana*   79

Drosera intermedia   80

Drosera tracyi   81

POWDERY STRAP AIR PLANT   83

CONSERVATION   85

Who Cares?   88

CULTIVATION'S ROLE IN CONSERVATION   89

SYBILLINE BOOKS   93

GROWING GUIDE   95

GLOSSARY   99

INDEX   101

ABOUT THE AUTHOR   103

"The fact that a plant should secrete, when properly excited, a fluid containing an acid and ferment, closely analogous to the digestive fluid of an animal, was certainly a remarkable discovery."

—Charles Darwin

MINDY LIGHTHIPE

Foreword

Welcome to the amazing world of carnivorous plants! This book will not only introduce you to these unique plants (they eat meat!) but also open your eyes to their evolutionary history and your role in their appreciation and conservation so that future generations can experience them.

Most of my youth was spent in the arid desert. I heard about weird plants called Venus flytraps on television or saw them in the pages of *National Geographic*. They seemed like alien beings from another world, a watery world in which plants could live in boggy conditions and hunt and consume prey.

My first in-person encounter with one of these beauties was *Sarracenia alata* (yellow trumpets) in coastal Mississippi. It was flowering throughout a seasonally flooded roadside field. Seeing the field while driving forty miles per hour, I thought it was a massive planting of daffodils, but I knew those plants didn't grow so far south. My curiosity was sparked, and a new world opened up to me!

And then I moved to Florida. Despite rampant development, Florida still has amazing natural lands that are home to a vast array of native plants and plant communities. There is so much intriguing natural history to learn and thousands of acres to explore. Once you realize the evolutionary **adaptations** that plants have made to survive their environments and predators, taking a hike can be like stepping back into ancient history.

It is both humbling and life-affirming to realize that many of Florida's native plants have been around a lot longer than we humans have. The complexity of their survival strategies—from the ways they communicate with other plants and organisms using chemicals to their flexible gender identification—wow!

I hope that you take the time to experience Florida's carnivorous plants in their natural habitats. The more you learn about something, the more likely you are to love and protect it. I hope that everyone who reads this book is inspired to save the last remaining tracts of wildness before they are paved over and destroyed forever.

—Juliet Rynear,
executive director of the Florida Native Plant Society

Preface

One day in AP biology class at Niagara Wheatfield High School in Niagara Falls, New York, we had a guest lecturer. He was the cryptic hall monitor. He went unbeknownst to students until they were caught being mischievous. On that day, Mr. Bruce Herman stepped up to the task of entertaining Mrs. Weber's six periods of bio. The topic was carnivorous plants, specifically their care. I had cared for a few Venus flytraps prior to his presentation, and all their verdant leaves had turned black within weeks.

As Mr. Herman explained, I quickly comprehended my multiple mistakes that had led to my plants' swift demise. Near the end of the presentation, he announced that he would be gifting Mrs. Weber's classroom with a terrarium and several *Nepenthes* for us to monitor throughout the school year. I was the only one, surprisingly, out of the 120 students, to show genuine interest. His passion captivated me. It revived my passion for plants. Until then, I was all about animals. And with my home pet population nearing capacity, I was sure my parents would be more receptive to a few carnivorous plants compared to another duck or goose.

For me, carnivorous plants represented some bizarre cross between botanical beauties and carnivorous animals. They are astonishing. I spoke to Mr. Herman after class and expressed my desire to own a Venus flytrap once again. But this time I would be able to keep it alive for years. The next day in the hall, he gifted me a Venus flytrap and a Cape sundew.

A few years later, in college, I met Ryan McGhee, who shared my botanical fascination. We wanted to share our enthusiasm for plants—specifically carnivorous ones—with the region. I knew exactly who to contact for more detailed growing information. Mr. Herman provided us with more specimen plants and taught us plant propagation techniques for carnivorous plants and daylilies. His mentorship allowed us to start the Western New York Carnivorous Plant Club. We met monthly over two years, and I presented on each of the common genera hobbyists grow. We had friendly competitions that led to further knowledge regarding each plant's optimum growing conditions.

Ryan and I moved to Florida, where we relished in all the things we could grow in our subtropical Tampa climate. I procured a Florida state nursery license and started selling carnivorous plants throughout central Florida. I was so successful I was able to use profits from my carnivorous plant business to pay for my master's degree in global sustainability. I wrote five TED-Ed Talks, including one on carnivorous plants that has been viewed over 1.5 million times. I then became active in the International Carnivorous Plant Society, serving on the board as the education director.

It's easy to undervalue the guidance and knowledge of a tranquil person. Thank you, Mr. Herman, for capturing my attention, which ultimately led to writing this book on Florida's carnivorous plants and their care.

Carnivorous Plants

A tiger's incisors, a cobra's venom, and an owl's talons are all adaptations for capturing and killing prey. These adaptations occurred over eons of evolution and turned these animals into precise predators. A hunter's adaptation is the result of competition and balance due to changing ecosystems and migration. The same is true of carnivorous plants.

All carnivorous plants have evolved modified leaves specialized for capturing and digesting prey to acquire nutrients. In addition to their ability to eat animals, one of the most fascinating details about carnivorous plants is that they are not closely related to each other. This means that carnivory in plants has evolved over millions of years, at different times and in different places, separately. These plants have descended from several different ancestors. We clump them all together because of their strange predatory method of gathering nutrients, but most of them are not closely genetically linked.

While most plants cannot live in the harsh habitats of bogs and swamps, carnivorous plants flourish there with their meat-eating adaptation. With other plants absent, carnivorous plants receive plenty of sunlight due to the lack of competition.

Wetlands, bogs, and swaps are usually stagnant bodies of water. This means no streams or rivers run through them. When plants die, they stay in the area and decompose. Since their acidic chemicals are not washed away, they pile up. Most microorganisms, which normally help break down dead plant matter, can't live in acidic conditions. Without decomposition, the dead plants do not turn into nutrients that living plants can use.

Other plants in nutrient-rich locations extract essential nutrients like nitrogen, phosphorus, and potassium through their roots. In nutrient-poor soils, plants that could benefit from the digestion of animals were able to survive. These plants passed on their traits to their offspring. With over seven hundred species of carnivorous plants found globally, we know that being able to digest insects and small animals has proven to be a useful adaptation.

Like other plants, carnivorous plants obtain their energy through photosynthesis. Green pigments called chlorophyll capture light energy and convert it into sugar. The sugar is then used by the plant as energy. What makes carnivorous plants different from traditional plants is that they are predators. They are not simply defending themselves; they are on the offense. Around the world, carnivorous plants kill animals—ranging from microscopic protozoa to rats—to acquire nutrients. These nutrients help them stay healthy, fight off pests and disease, and grow into mature plants capable of reproduction.

Although carnivorous plants have descended from several different ancestors and are not necessarily related, they do share some traits. For a plant to be considered carnivorous, biologists generally say that the plant can capture and kill prey, is able to digest the prey, and benefit from the digested nutrients. But noncarnivorous plants can do some of these things as well. What is and what is not a carnivorous plant is a sacred topic, not a scientific one—thus the debate.

Plants that don't have all three of the above traits are sometimes referred to as semicarnivorous or paracarnivorous. In environments with lots of nutrients found in the ground, being able to catch and digest bugs is generally not helpful, as it requires energy to move and make traps and produce digestive enzymes. In these environments noncarnivorous plants would outcompete carnivorous ones by growing taller faster.

While most carnivorous plants will grow without eating prey, they may not thrive. Carnivorous plants that get nutrients from prey grow larger and are healthier. If you care for carnivorous plants in your house or backyard, it is a good idea to provide them with snacks. You can do this by growing them outside or by hand-feeding them insects.

Carnivorous plants generally need more water than most other terrestrial plants; this is especially true of those native to Florida. Many carnivorous plants (including Venus flytraps, North American pitcher plants, bladderworts, and many sundews) do well in the tray method, where potted plants sit in a tray of water. We'll talk more about this as we explore Florida's genera of carnivorous plants.

CARNIVOROUS PLANTS HAVE EVOLVED TO LIVE IN MANY DIFFERENT HABITATS, NOT ONLY IN FLORIDA BUT AROUND THE WORLD.

Drosera intermedia. ALEX ROUKAS

Drosera filiformis var. *floridana.* MANNY HERRERA

Catopsis berteroniana. CELINE LEROY

Carnivorous Plant Life Cycle

Angiosperms are plants that produce flowers, which when pollinated produce seeds. These fertilized seeds grow into new plants. All carnivorous plants are classified as angiosperms and can produce seeds. In addition to growing new plants from seeds, gardeners can also grow new plants using several additional methods.

All carnivorous plants are angiosperms and produce flowers, like these *Utricularia resupinata* in the Webb Wildlife Management Area in Charlotte County, Florida. ALAN CRESSLER

Propagation Methods of Carnivorous Plants

Sexual (Seed)	Asexual (Vegetative)
Hybrid—a plant that was produced by crossing two plants of different species or cultivars. Gardeners will take pollen from one plant and rub it on the stigma of another plant. This is called pollination. It's not too difficult. Bees do this accidentally all the time.	Cuttings—many carnivorous plants can be multiplied by taking pieces of their leaves or stems and placing them in damp soil or water. Once they form roots, these cuttings can be transferred into a pot, where they will grow a clone of the original plant.
	Division—pulling a rhizome apart can create two or more plants.
Purebred—a plant that was produced by parents of the same species or cultivar.	Micropropagation—this is the practice of multiplying plants from small pieces of almost any plant part, including anthers, petals, pollen, stem tips, or tissue. Sometimes only a single cell is needed!
	Plantlets—some plants produce baby plants at the end of their stems or leaves. Press these plantlets into soil. Once they develop roots, separate them from the parent and place them in their own pot.

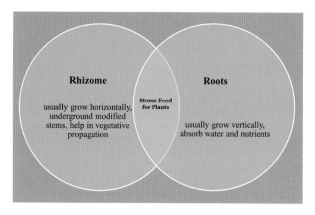

Rhizome

usually grow horizontally, underground modified stems, help in vegetative propagation

Stores Food for Plants

Roots

usually grow vertically, absorb water and nutrients

Many carnivorous plants that you'll want to keep are from areas of the world that have a range of temperatures throughout the year. The Venus flytrap, for example, is native to the Carolinas, which experience chilly winters. North American pitcher plants (*Sarracenia*) in their native environment also experience mild to warm summers and freezing winters. These plants are called temperate plants. Temperate plants do best when they are given time to go into dormancy. Like animals going into hibernation, dormancy is a survival tactic. When daylight and temperature decrease, plants cannot perform photosynthesis. During the cooler months, these plants will lose leaves and stop growing. Do *not* throw them away! They are simply resting. Many customers have told me they have composted what they thought were dead plants in the fall. I believe they have thrown away healthy plants that were dormant. In the spring, they will wake up from dormancy and start growing again. Many carnivorous plants are perennials. Perennials take more than two years to reach maturity. *Sarracenia* take three to five years to mature. Venus flytraps take four to five years to mature and can live over twenty years. You can keep them indefinitely if you continually separate offshoots.

With proper care, this *Dionaea* 'Fused Tooth' can live over twenty years.

Annuals, like radishes, reach maturity within one season. Carrots are examples of biennials, which take two years to complete their growing cycle. Venus flytraps, take more than two years to reach maturity and are classified as perennials.

If the amount of light and heat a temperate plant receives does not decrease, the plant usually weakens and may die. Dormancy allows plants to rest. In the Growing Carnivorous Plants section, we will discuss ways to mimic dormancy in your house.

PLANT VERSUS ANIMAL DIGESTION

Most carnivorous plants use digestive enzymes to break down their meals. Digestive enzymes are protein molecules that help speed up the chemical reaction that turns the prey into nutrients that can be used by the plants.

Your salvia has digestive enzymes in it. Animals and carnivorous plants produce different types of digestive enzymes. Each helps break down different nutrients. We humans have amylase, which breaks down carbohydrates and starches; protease, which handles proteins; and lipase, which works on fats.

Scientists have found in carnivorous plants these three digestive enzymes as well as at least a dozen others, like chitinase, esterase, peroxidase, phosphatase, and ribonuclease.

EVOLUTION

Carnivorous plants evolved independently around nine times. When sunlight, water, and nutrients—the basic elements plants need to survive—are jumbled, "life, uh, finds a way," as Dr. Ian Malcolm in *Jurassic Park* eloquently describes. Plants whose random mutations enabled them to extract nutrients from insects, rather than the soil, thrived. And it was not until recently that we understood how.

Many carnivorous plants go through a period of dormancy. Don't throw them away. Trim off the dead leaves and wait for spring.

A carnivorous plant takes in nutrients from prey, which in turn gives the plant an advantage for growing or reproducing. Carnivorous plants also must actively lure, attract, and trap their prey.

When studying an organism's origin story, most biologists look at fossils. Fossils can show how organisms have changed over time. Fossils are usually formed by the hard parts of organisms, such as bark, bones, teeth, and shells. Since carnivorous plants do not have those, only a few fossils of them exist. Using molecular clock models based on determining the mutation rates of biomolecules, it is estimated that some carnivorous plants evolved ninety-five million years ago and others as recently as 1.9 million years ago. Scientists agree that there isn't one single origin story for all carnivorous plants.

Venus flytraps and sundews shared a common ancestor sixty million years ago, while pitcher plants of North and South America originated around forty-eight million years ago. Biologists who have studied the genes of Venus flytraps have learned they are closely related to sundews. Venus flytraps and sundews produce the same type of acid to kill their victims. The most recent botanical carnivores evolved in the bromeliad family around 1.9 million years ago. Today carnivorous plants are found on every continent except Antarctica. Florida has more carnivorous *Utricularias* plant species than any other state. We'll talk about why Florida is a hotspot of biodiversity in the section Florida's Carnivorous Plants.

Noncarnivorous plants can absorb fertilizer through their leaves. This is known as "foliar feeding." If plants can benefit from absorbing nutrients through their leaves, you can imagine that over millions of years, leaves that happen to have hairs that could catch raindrops and nutrients would have an advantage. If an insect died in the liquid, the plants would have an even bigger advantage. These plants with more hairs would outcompete their neighbors and pass on their traits to their offspring, just like how you acquired traits from your mother and father. Plants that happen to have inward-curved leaves that collect and funnel nutrients would have an advantage over those that had outward-curved leaves.

Pitcher plants create proteins to protect themselves against attackers such as fungi. Fungi support their cell walls with chitin. Chitin is also the basis of arthropod exoskeletons. So proteins that were first used to fight fungal parasites eventually become chitinase, the chemical that breaks down insects. Plants that were able to repurpose their molecules had an advantage over those that did not. Today, *Sarracenia*, *Nepenthes*, and *Cephalotus* (three types of pitcher plants) have chitinase in their digestive enzymes at the base of their pitcher, which breaks down their meals.

Although North American pitcher plants, Asian pitcher plants, and Australian pitcher plants all have a common name and similar trapping methods and digestive enzymes, they evolved independently from one another. This is called convergent evolution. These three pitcher plant families are separated by millions of years of evolution. The Australian pitcher plant is more closely related to the noncarnivorous starfruit tree than it is to the other pitcher plants.

Since carnivorous plants are indeed plants, they must get nitrogen and phosphorus by some means. And evolution has a compromise. Carnivorous plant leaves that trap animals are less efficient for photosynthesizing than regular leaves. Unfortunately, the more trapping leaves, the fewer photosynthesizing leaves a plant can have. This means they have fewer photosynthesizing leaves than a regular plant and generally need to live in areas that have a lot of sunlight. This is why Venus flytraps and many sun-loving Florida carnivorous plants are not doing well now—they are being shaded by larger noncarnivorous plants and can't compete.

TAXONOMY

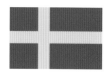

Taxonomy is the part of science that names and classifies organisms. In the early 1700s, Swedish scientist Carl Linnaeus created a way to name and organize species that we still use today. He created a two-part naming system for all living things that helped reduce misunderstanding. Since many carnivorous plants eat flies, people in different parts of the world, with different languages, may be confused when discussing flytraps. But when people refer to a plant as *Dionaea muscipula*, they can be sure they are referencing the same plant. Using Latin (and sometimes Greek), Linnaeus was able to standardize the naming of species for all scientists. Latin was a good choice because it is a dead language, so it is not constantly changing, and it is a universal choice, with no countries being able to claim taxonomy.

The other reason why the Linnaean system worked so well is that he grouped organisms by similarities and not just differences. Linnaean taxonomy—or scientific classification, as it is known today—uses a hierarchy. The kingdom level contains organisms that are grouped very broadly. They have some similarities but a lot of differences. As you go down the taxonomic ladder, the specificity increases. His binomial system included a first name, or genus, which represented a general category, and a species name based on precise characteristics. The genus is always written with a capital letter, followed by the species, which is written in lowercase. Once an author has fully written out the genus, they may choose to just write the first letter. For example, since I've already written *Dionaea muscipula* in this section, I may now refer to it as *D. muscipula*. The genus and species are in italics to distinguish them as an identified species. Taxonomic group levels that are above genus are written in standard roman type.

Two Forms of Taxonomy

Taxonomy as You Were Taught in School	A *Slightly* More Realistic View of How Taxonomists Classify Plants	
Kingdom	Kingdom	
	Subkingdom	
	Superdivision	
Phylum	Division	
Class	Class	
	Subclass	
Order	Order	
Family	Family	
Genus	Genus	
Species	Species	
	Subspecies	Variety or Cultivar
	Form	

On the right side of the previous table, I left out a few levels and did not mention clades, but you get the idea that taxonomy is a complicated science. While you may be familiar with the higher levels of classification, the bottom section, where botanists really split up plants and put them in their own category, can be confusing.

Botanists and biologists use varying degrees for what classifies as a species. In general, a species is a group of organisms that can reproduce with each other and produce fertile offspring that in turn resemble their parents. This is a sufficient definition for zoology. When tigers and lions or donkeys and horses mate, they produce infertile offspring.

Therefore, it's easy to label them as separate species. But in the botanical world, species of *Sarracenia*, *Drosera*, grapes, roses, violets, and many others can hybridize within their genera. They can produce fertile offspring, making the previous definition inadequate. Using German-born evolutionary biologist Ernst Mayr's definition "groups of actually or potentially interbreeding natural populations that are reproductively isolated from other such groups" is definitely more appropriate for plants—and good for African lions and Asian tigers too.

A subspecies is a group within a species used to describe organisms that are geographically isolated. If they could interact with each other, they would produce viable offspring.

The taxonomic distinction *variety* includes organisms within a species that have a special trait but are not geographically separated. For example, in Florida we have the parrot pitcher plant: *Sarracenia psittacina*. In some parts of its range, there is a huge variant. These extra-large and in charge plants are known as *Sarracenia psittacina* var. *okefenokeensis*. Now that scientists have recognized a subgroup of the main population, the remaining plants get the **autonym** name. That is, all the "normal" plants are now automatically called *Sarracenia psittacina* subsp. *psittacina*.

Karen Henningsen holds a typical *Sarracenia psittacina* subsp. *psittacina*, while Bruce Bednar holds a *Sarracenia psittacina* var. *okefenokeensis*, which he affectionately calls 'Golfballensis' and a regular-size *Sarracenia psittacina* all-green variety known as 'Alba'.

The taxonomic rung of *form* is the most discriminatory. If there is a tiny distinction and the scientist does not believe it to have evolutionary significance, they may designate it with an official name that includes the form. In the giant parrot pitcher plants, there are a few that are anthocyanin-free, which leads to an all-green giant parrot pitcher plant. Its official scientifically recognized name is *Sarracenia psittacina* var. *okefenokeensis* f. *luteoviridis*.

And now we get to the point where you may ask yourself, "Who cares?" I definitely did while doing research for this book. One major reason why taxonomy is important is because it is closely associated with conservation. Although describing the world's species and their evolutionary relationships is not the same as saving them, it does help lawmakers and activists know where to go and what to save. On its own, a list of every species, subspecies, and form within a region will do nothing to help conserve a species. While different botanists have various perspectives on what exactly a species is, once it is published as a distinct evolutionary unit, conservation efforts can be put into place. Lobbyists can then argue for saving the plants or habitats, since they represent a distinct subset of biodiversity and are therefore of heightened conservation value. Effective management depends on understanding the activities causing their decline, creating effective management policies, and successfully implementing them.

One problem that biologists face is how to identify what is an **evolutionarily significant unit (ESU)**. Initially scientists suggested that the group of organisms should be "substantially reproductively isolated." A famous rhetorical example is that while squirrels in Central Park are reproductively isolated from other squirrel populations, does that warrant their protection? Probably not.

Now scientists have added a second standard for looking at ESUs. It must also represent "an important component in the evolutionary legacy of the species."

A conference of zoo biologists in 1985 created the term *ESU*. Since zoos have limited space, saving two of every kind is not feasible. With a growing population of humans, we are also running out of habitable space for many species of carnivorous plants. Consider *Sarracenia rubra*. In Florida we have *Sarracenia rubra* subsp. *gulfensis* and *Sarracenia rubra* subsp. *wherryi*. While there is a small overlap in the counties in Florida where they occur, they most likely do not occur at the same site. If a real estate developer wants to build a cul-de-sac, lawmakers need to decide if the section of land where the last remaining subspecies of *Sarracenia rubra* live merits protection. Some may argue that different subspecies of *Sarracenia rubra* live elsewhere and that plants that have a special color or a distinct size are not worthy of conservation.

A stand of *Sarracenia flava* varieties in Liberty County, Florida.
MANNY HERRERA

Now consider this: *Sarracenia rubra* subsp. *wherryi* goes by another name according to some scientists: *Sarracenia alabamensis* subsp. *wherryi*. Same plant, different name (this is further discussed in the North American Pitcher Plant chapter). *Sarracenia alabamensis* is a critically endangered plant. Will that cause a different outcome about where to build?

Biodiversity leads to resiliency. Ensuring the protection of variations within a species is a form of insurance. We should want to increase populations that are unique. This leads to long-term preservation. Environmental factors contribute to subspecies differences. Hypothetically, consider a subspecies of *Sarracenia* that has a larger mouth. This trait could be favorable in environments where there are large bugs but small populations of them. Thus, the plants can compensate for the small population by eating a few large insects, which will allow the plants to acquire sufficient nutrients. This could eventually lead to other changes in the genes. If these changes eventually lead to preventing the plant from breeding with the other subspecies, we would declare a new species.

When reviewing wild plants or deciding what plants to add to your collection, it is important to research them based on their genus and species name to make sure you are studying the right plant.

How Plants and Animals Are Named

Almost fifteen thousand new species of plants and animals are discovered every year. While there is a formal code of conduct when naming organisms, scientists like to have fun. All scientific names must use letters of the Latin alphabet, the name must be unique, and it isn't official until the name is published. Check out these creative names.

Aha ha	Arnold Menke named this Australian wasp after winning a debate regarding the validity of the species, in which he allegedly exclaimed, "Aha ha!"
Aptostichus barackobamai	Californian spider named after President Barack Obama.
Aptostichus stephencolberti	Californian spider named after comedian Stephen Colbert.
Ba humbugi	Species of land snail named after a phrase attributed to fictional character Ebenezer Scrooge.
Carmenelectra	Genus of extinct fly found in Baltic amber named after the model and actress Carmen Electra.
Irritator challengeri	Named after the Brazilian dinosaur that caused the paleontologists much grief.
Mephitis mephitis	Named for the common striped skunk, which translates to "smelliest of the smelly."
Nepenthes attenboroughii	Pitcher plant named after naturalist Sir David Attenborough.
Preseucoela imallshookupis	Species of gall wasp with the genus named after Elvis Presley and the species named after his song "All Shook Up."
Pieza deresistans, Pieza kake, Pieza pi, Pieza rhea	Bugologist Neal Evenhuis in 2002 named these mythicomyiid flies. *Pieza rhea* (scrub pygmy bee fly) is only found in seven sites on the Lake Wales Ridge, Florida.
Spongiforma squarepantsii	Malaysian species of fungus named after the yellow cartoon sponge.

Florida's Carnivorous Plants

Due to our current seasonal variability in the northern part of the state and the stability created by tropics in the south, Florida is home to more carnivorous plants than any other state. The Everglades, for example, is a unique habitat in Florida and provides us with some spectacular species. This subtropical climate, with a broad shallow river, creates a unique environment that supports a large diversity of plants and animals—some of which are carnivorous plants. In the southern part of the state, which encompasses the Everglades, you can find several species of *Utricularia*, *Pinguicula pumila*, and the endangered carnivorous bromeliad *Catopsis berteroniana*.

The panhandle of Florida is home to even more species of carnivorous plants. You can find additional species of *Pinguicula* as well as *Drosera*, *Sarracenia*, and the non-native Venus flytrap. Dr. Alex Eilts, an ecologist with the University of Minnesota, presents a detailed explanation of why we have this hotspot of biodiversity in his video titled *Glacier Stragglers*.

When glaciers last coated North America, this region functioned as a haven from the freezing temperatures that were occurring farther north. Florida was protected from the severe weather by the warm waters of the Gulf of Mexico. Many species that took refuge in the panhandle

The endangered carnivorous bromeliad *Catopsis berteroniana*. CELINE LEROY

have now repopulated the eastern temperate forests. While some species were able to recolonize the southern United States, others are now trapped in the very area that served as a refuge for them some twenty thousand years ago.

Back then, a huge continental glacier covered all of Canada and most of the northern United States as far south as the Ohio river valley. The northern part of the continent was too cold for many temperate species. Two species of giant ground sloths grazed on the tundra of Tennessee! During the late Pleistocene (often referred to as the Ice Age), the Great Smoky Mountains region was also home to species of mammoths, peccaries, bears, large-toothed cats, tapir, caribou, and elk. Of the thirty-some species of megafauna that were present back then, only five remain today.

South of that region were boreal forests or snow forests, like those in northern Canada today. Boreal forests are categorized as having coniferous forests with freezing temperatures occurring for six to eight months a year. During the glacial periods, the sea level lowered by three hundred feet, causing Florida to double in size. Warmer periods (with higher sea levels) caused the peninsula to shrink in size.

Twenty thousand years ago, the panhandle of Florida was the sweet spot for temperate species. Its combination of warm and wet was ideal for those species to grow. As the glaciers melted and retreated north, some species followed. Pioneering species were those that were able to withstand the harsh open landscape. This included being able to tolerate fire. And while it may seem strange, wildfires are common in many types of ecosystems. They are even necessary for some plants to grow. Long leaf pines, for example, favored these harsh prehistoric conditions. They were able to take over the landscape due to their unique grass stage, which has evolved to be fire-tolerant. Those plants that could bounce back after being burned survived and passed on their fire-tolerant traits to their offspring. Fire is important to so many environments that it's an entire field of study within ecology, with an international association putting out peer-reviewed articles on the subject multiple times a year.

The absence of fire can have as much of an effect on the environment as a wildfire. The environment and the life cycle of organisms determine when fires return and their magnitude. This happens in every ecosystem. When people employ fire-suppression efforts, this disrupts the natural fire cycle and can change the makeup of the forest. *Sarracenia* and Venus flytraps, for example, need a lot of sunlight. When fires are suppressed, brush and trees grow quickly and block out the sun the carnivorous plants depend on.

These *Sarracenia minor* were spotted under power lines in Volusia County, Florida. The mowing mimics naturally occurring fires, which prevents woody plants from shading them out. MANNY HERRARA

Since there are fire-suppression efforts in Florida, under power lines and on roadsides are great places to find carnivorous plants because the mowing mimics fire. Both mowing and fire control woody plants and keep them from shading out native grasses and carnivorous plants. In some of Florida's pine flatwoods and savannas, controlled fires do occur. Without frequent fires, these open, sunny habitats will become dense thickets of vegetation. Carnivorous plants will not grow well when they are shaded. Although they will appear weak, stretching for the sun, most will recover after a fire clears out their competitors.

Plants that migrated here for the moderate weather so many years ago are now stuck here since they cannot tolerate the cold temperatures farther north. What still puzzles scientists is why some other species can expand their range and recolonize while others are geographically restricted to the Florida glacial refuge. Many *Sarracenia* species can be found in the Gulf Coastal Plains, while some species extend their range to the west or northeast. One species, *Sarracenia purpurea*, has recolonized all the way up to Canada.

Since most of the *Sarracenia* species' range overlaps in the panhandle of Florida, this leads to areas of high biodiversity. *Pinguicula*—the butterworts—are an even better example of how species overlapping in range lead to biodiversity hotspots.

The most shocking part of Dr. Eilts's explanation of Florida's biodiversity hotspot is the time scale. The majority of species were unable to recolonize in twenty thousand years. Now think about today's climate. Consider all those species that will not be able to respond to the rapid change in a few hundred years. Plants and animals can and do adapt to climate change over many generations. However, if the climate changes too rapidly, many will go extinct.

The beautiful flower color variants in *Pinguicula pumila*. Photo taken in St. Joseph Bay State Buffer Preserve, Florida.
JEAN MENGELKOCH

DRAINING THE SWAMP

Does it trouble anyone that people flock to central Florida to visit a fake swamp that was built on top of a real one? In the early 1960s, the Orlando region was mostly swampland with some interstate highways being developed. When the movie-making mogul Walt Disney flew over this cheap land, he decided to build his East Coast amusement park near the Florida turnpike and nearby airport. To make the most magical place on earth, dozens of canals and levees were created to drain an entire lake. A year after the amusement park's opening, Congress passed the Clean Water Act. This act recognized the importance of wetlands. They filter our water and provide habitats for many organisms. Part of the law mandated builders to restore nearby areas whenever they drained or paved over wetlands.

In the 1990s, to expand the park, Disney purchased a huge tract of land and donated it to the non-profit Nature Conservancy. Today, on the Nature Conservancy's website, they claim that "the Nature Conservancy's 11,500-acre Disney Wilderness Preserve near Kissimmee stands as a testament not only to Disney's love of nature, but also to the power of cooperation, perseverance and innovative thinking." Let us not forget that the Walt Disney Company also did it because it was required by law.

Today, you can visit the Orlando area and ride on a boat over a man-made river or travel a little farther south in the state and experience the real Florida. Well, sort of.

WOMEN'S WORK

"It is a woman's business to be interested in the environment. It's an extended form of housekeeping."

—Marjory Stoneman Douglas

Draining the swamps of Florida has a long history that goes back to way before the famous mouse pulled the drain. In the mid-1700s, maps referred to Florida's peninsula as mostly islands. This could be true, since the water level in the Everglades then was six to eight feet higher than it is now. In the area formerly known as Laguna del Espiritu Santo (The Lagoon of the Holy Spirit), Franciscan monks were told by the Native Americans that they could paddle their canoes from coast to coast.

Between 1881 and 1927, many governmental officials and businessmen attempted to pump out the Everglades. Many projects started, and all failed; then bigger and better projects started, and they also failed. It took two devastating hurricanes in 1926 and 1928 for the Army Corps of Engineers to focus on not draining the Everglades but instead trying to keep the surrounding farmland from flooding. Although they couldn't drain the Everglades, people have drastically altered its ecosystems. Today the Everglades is less than half its original size. One reason the current situation is not worse is because it is a difficult task to drain four thousand square miles of wetlands. The second reason is because a handful of dedicated women fought to preserve the wetlands.

Canal being dredged by steam shovel for the Everglades drainage project in 1906. FLORIDA MEMORY

Dredge "Culebra" on the St. Lucie Canal in the Everglades Drainage District. The Everglades Drainage District was established in 1913 for the purpose of draining and reclaiming lands located near the Everglades for agricultural and sanitary purposes. To carry out this mandate, a system of canals, drains, levees, dikes, dams, locks, and reservoirs was constructed. Photographed in September 1921. FLORIDA MEMORY

WATCHFUL WAITING

FLORIDA EVERGLADES

This 1916 cartoon shows potential settlers and businessmen awaiting "progress." Published in a booklet made by attorney James M. Carson for the Back to Broward League. The league derived its name from Florida governor Napoleon Bonaparte Broward, who had led drainage efforts. FLORIDA MEMORY

In 1904, Napoleon Bonaparte Broward saw the Florida wilderness as something that humans could and should control. His slogan to win the governorship was "Water will run downhill!" He wanted to drain the Everglades for agriculture purposes. He thought the newly exposed land could allow farmers to create a Jeffersonian agrarian utopia.

Frank Stoneman also saw the Everglades as a wasteland but thought it was too big to be transformed for human use. As editor of a Miami newspaper, he criticized Broward's drainage plan for being impractical and inefficient.

In 1915, May Mann Jennings, as president of the Florida Federation of Women's Clubs and chairwoman of the Preservation Committee, secured legislation establishing the Royal Palm State Park, near Homestead. Nicknamed the "Mother of Florida Forestry," Jennings was known for her political and social shrewdness. The Paradise Key area was first surveyed in the mid-1800s and was celebrated for its botanical diversity and **hammock**. Concerned that this area was going to be developed, Jennings took an interest in the land and began campaigning for the area to be declared a state park. Its establishment started a larger conservation effort that led to the founding of the Everglades National Park.

First lady of Florida May Mann Jennings, photographed in 1901. FLORIDA MEMORY

15

Around the same time, Minnie Moore-Willson advocated for the Seminole and Miccosukee people, who had been pushed into the boggy Everglades region as white settlers established towns throughout the state. Moore-Willson's support for the indigenous people living in the wetlands was unpopular at the time. Most Floridians wanted the Native Americans to assimilate into American culture. She instead immersed herself into theirs. Moore-Willson understood that the fates of the Seminoles and the Everglades were intertwined. She opposed the draining of the Everglades as business and real estate tycoons vied for the chance to tame the swamp and turn it into something "useful."

Due to Moore-Willson's commitment to the Seminole culture, she contributed to the passing of the Florida Seminole Land bill, which preserved one hundred thousand acres of undrained Everglades land for Seminole use. In 1934, the Seminoles traded their area for a reservation in Hollywood, Florida, since the park would have prohibited them from hunting.

In Moore-Willson's book *The Birds of the Everglades and Their Neighbors the Seminole Indians*, she writes, "An Everglade Preserve would not only protect and save the remnant of America's wildlife, but would have an educational effect, not to Florida alone, but also to the thousands of visitors from other states. It would be of great economic value to America. It would become a world-famed tribute to the Land of Flowers."

Marjory Stoneman Douglas began working for her father, Frank Stoneman, at the *Miami Herald* in 1915. She wrote about and lobbied for feminism, racial justice, migrant farm workers' conditions, and conservation before these topics were in vogue. In the 1920s, she became involved in the Everglades through serving on the board of the Everglades Tropical National Park Committee. During the 1930s, she wrote a pamphlet on a botanical garden, sparking the interest of several South Florida gardening clubs who then asked her to guest lecture. Voted "class orator" of Wellesley College in Massachusetts, she further honed her public speaking skills through these clubs.

In the 1940s, Douglas spent five years researching the Everglades, the ecosystems of which were not well understood. In November 1947, she published her book *The Everglades: River of Grass*, which described the region's river as not only worthy of conservation but as unavoidably connected to Florida's citizens and traditions. She was a highly skilled advocate for the Everglades and in 1947 fought against both Big Sugar and the Corps of Engineers, who had planned on diverting the water or polluting it. The Everglades National Park was established later that year.

Known for her ability to tame the wildest of crowds, at five foot two inches, Douglas could not only command a crowd but also engage, inspire, and empower them. A notorious example of Douglas's presenting wit is when she was presenting the harmful practices of the Army Corps of Engineers at a community meeting. A colonel dropped his pen, and as he bent over to pick it up, Douglas said, "Colonel! You can crawl under that table and hide, but you can't get away from me!"

John Rothchild, in his introduction to Douglas's autobiography *Voice of the River*, said, "She reminded us all of our responsibility to nature and I don't remember what else. Her voice had the sobering effect of a one-room schoolmarm's. The tone itself seemed to tame the rowdiest of the local stone crabbers, plus the developers, and the lawyers on both sides. I wonder if it didn't also intimidate the mosquitoes."

With the Everglades still under attack by Big Agriculture, Big Sugar, and urban sprawl in 1969, at age seventy-nine, Douglas formed the group Friends of the Everglades. She served as the head of the organization. Her purpose was to create awareness of the potential destruction to a large portion of the Everglades by a huge jetport then being constructed. While one runway was built, the jetport project was prevented. Spending the rest of her life protecting the Everglades, she believed that the people who pollute the Everglades should clean it up. Today the Everglades hosts one-third of the state's carnivorous plant species.

Marjory Stoneman Douglas signing autographs at a Burdines department store in Miami, Florida, 1948. FLORIDA MEMORY

16

Marjory Stoneman Douglas's Legacy

1980	The Florida Department of Natural Resources (now the Florida Department of Environmental Protection) names its headquarters in Tallahassee after her.
1991	Queen Elizabeth II visits Douglas and is gifted a signed copy of her book *The Everglades: River of Grass*.
	Douglas requests that trees be planted instead of giving gifts and holding celebrations for her hundred and second birthday. Over one hundred thousand trees are planted across Florida, and a bald cypress is added to the lawn of the governor's mansion.
1993	President Bill Clinton awards Douglas the Presidential Medal of Freedom. The quote for the medal reads, "Marjory Stoneman Douglas personifies passionate commitment. Her crusade to preserve and restore the Everglades has enhanced our Nation's respect for our precious environment, reminding all of us of nature's delicate balance. Grateful Americans honor the 'Grandmother of the Glades' by following her splendid example in safeguarding America's beauty and splendor for generations to come."
1997	Over a million acres of the Everglades National Park is christened the Marjory Stoneman Douglas Wilderness.
1999	She is posthumously inducted into the National Wildlife Federation Hall of Fame.
2000	She is posthumously inducted into the National Women's Hall of Fame.

SCIENTIFIC PROGRESS

For hundreds—maybe thousands—of years, people have been fascinated by carnivorous plants. The famous naturalist Charles Darwin published his 1875 book on them, titled *Insectivorous Plants*, after he studied them for nearly a decade.

Textbooks and education systems focus on Darwin because before his understanding and explanation of change over time through natural selection, many people thought that organisms where immutable—that is, unchanging. During the scientific revolution and enlightenment era, there was no such thing as *biology*. That term wasn't used until 1799. Instead, the observation-based study of living things was called natural history.

Maria Sibylla Merian, a German-born naturalist, was the prominent entomologist of the late 1600s and became famous for studying metamorphosis. She raised butterflies and caterpillars at home, and she traveled to South America in 1699 to study the insects of the jungles of Suriname. In total she studied, reported, and illustrated close to two hundred insect species. Merian's detailed reports became the benchmark for other natural historians. What is more remarkable, however, is that her observations helped dispel the popular belief that insects spontaneously emerged from mud!

Carl Linnaeus was another pre-Darwinian scientist who helped Darwin and us today see how organisms are related. He wanted to compare all species with each other to get a better understanding of the natural world. While other scientists were also trying to come up with methods of classifying organisms, his system won out, and it is the one we still use today—even though there have been many changes.

While Linnaeus did not travel and collect organisms, he was able to classify and name over twelve thousand species. Some of them have been renamed, but nevertheless this is a very impressive life's work. Unfortunately, the mechanism by which he was able to examine so many species in such a short time is distressing—it was due to colonialism.

Sir Joseph Banks, for example, after voyaging to Brazil, Tahiti, New Zealand, and Australia, returned to England to great fame. He then advised King George III on the creation of the Kew Royal Botanical Gardens. He sent botanists around the world to bring back exotic species that would make Kew noteworthy. He is credited for procuring (using military force, most likely) around thirty thousand plants for the botanical gardens. These plants were grown, studied, and classified.

John Ellis, a British naturalist, christened the Venus flytrap with its scientific name *Dionaea muscipula* (Dione's mousetrap) and hypothesized that not only did it snap shut but that it was insectivorous. When he sent his idea and dried specimens to Carl Linnaeus, Linnaeus declared "to think that plants ate insects would go against the order of nature as willed by God."

Sarracenia flava var. *ornata* showing off at Kew Royal Botanical Gardens.

Nearly one hundred years later, we get to Charles Darwin. Victorian England was interested in Gothic forms of art, literature, and exotic botanical beauties. After much research, Darwin's dark description of the plant world in his book *Insectivorous Plants* pre-sold 1,700 of the 1,250 available copies in the first printing.

In 1984, Tom Givnish, born in Philadelphia, Pennsylvania, wrote a new definition of what a carnivorous plant is. This description is what many use today. A plant must have two basic requirements to be considered carnivorous. First, it must be able to absorb nutrients from dead prey. This absorption of nutrients must add some increment to fitness in terms of increased growth, pollen production, or seed set. This distinguishes carnivory from plants that have a defensive adaptation. Plants that immobilize or kill animals to aid in plant survival but do not absorb their nutrients are not considered carnivorous.

Second, to be considered carnivorous, the plant must have some type of adaptation or resource allocation that actively attracts, captures, and/or digests prey. This trait is required for differentiation because many plants can passively benefit by absorbing nutrients from dead animals decaying in the soil or on the surface of leaves.

ECOSYSTEMS
In addition to the Everglades, Florida is home to many exceptional ecosystems.

Florida's Carnivorous Plants Inhabit Many Unique Ecosystems

Name	Description	Location
Backwater	Part of a river with little or no current. Can occur in a branch of a main river or in the body of the main river where an obstruction has occurred.	Statewide
Basin swamp	Usually a large basin wetland with peat substrate that is seasonally flooded.	Panhandle to central peninsula
Cypress stringers	Narrow linear swamps dominated by pond cypress (*Taxodium ascendens*).	Panhandle
Depression marsh	Small, isolated depressions in sand substrate with peat gathering in the center; surrounded by fire-maintained community; seasonally flooded.	Statewide excluding Keys
Dome swamp	Shallow, isolated depression in sand/marl/limestone substrate with peat accumulating toward center; occurring within a fire-maintained community; seasonally inundated; still water.	Statewide excluding Keys
Mesic flatwoods	Flatland with sand substrate; mesic; frequent fire (every two to four years); open pine canopy with a layer of low shrubs and herbs.	Statewide excluding extreme southern peninsula and Keys
Seepage slope wetlands	On or at the base of a slope with loamy sand substrate; maintained by downslope seepage; usually saturated but rarely inundated.	Panhandle and northern peninsula

Name	Description	Location
Seepage stream	Perennial or intermittent seasonal waterways originating from shallow ground waters that have percolated through deep, sandy, upland soils. Typically have clear to lightly colored water maintained at fairly constant temperatures of around 70°F. Synonyms: pitcher plant bog, seepage bog	Panhandle to southern peninsula
Swamp lake	Generally shallow, open-water area within basin swamps; still water or flowthrough; peat, sand, or clay substrate; variable water chemistry but characteristically highly colored, acidic, soft water with moderate mineral content (sodium, chloride, sulfate); very little nutrients to rich in nutrients.	Statewide excluding Keys
Wet flatwoods	Pine forests with a sparse or absent midstory and a dense groundcover of hydrophytic grasses, herbs, and low shrubs. Synonym: wetland pine savanna	Statewide excluding extreme southern peninsula and Keys
Wet prairies	Flatland with sand or clay-sand substrate; usually saturated but only occasionally inundated.	Statewide excluding extreme southern peninsula and Keys

SOURCE: FLORIDA NATURAL AREAS INVENTORY

Sarracenia leucophylla in Franklin County, Florida. KAREN HENNINGSEN

Growing Carnivorous Plants

The lure of growing carnivorous plants is strong. In addition to their insectivorous habits, their unique shapes and colors add value to any backyard garden or windowsill. Having diverged from traditional plants millions of years ago, carnivorous plants require some special care. Luckily, Florida's species require very similar husbandry. Once you learn how to grow one, you'll be able to apply that knowledge and confidence to a wide range of flesh-eating botanical beauties.

BOGS AND CONTAINERS

When choosing a container, select plastic or glazed. Plastic pots last a long time and are inexpensive. Many of the common Florida carnivorous plant species and hybrids fluctuate their growth habit throughout the year. Therefore, repotting is not needed as often as a tropical house plant. When customers purchase a plant in a three-inch plastic pot and it does not need to be repotted for several years, I recommend setting the nursery pot within a more decorative one without drainage. This solution saves the customer time and money. Clay pots that have been glazed are heavy and durable but can be expensive. While a very few carnivorous plants can handle the chemical compounds found in terra-cotta pots, no Florida species can manage. Terra-cotta pots cause salts and minerals to build up to toxic levels in the soil. These pots also are absorbent and cause the soil to dry out.

If you inset your plastic pot into a decorative coffee mug or container that does not have a drainage hole, keep the water level at one-quarter to one-half an inch. If you are keeping the plant in the plastic nursery pot, use the standard tray method to water your plants. Get a dish that holds water,

"It's a Trap!" JOHN BRUEGGEN

Unlike most houseplants, many carnivorous plants will appreciate sitting in one-quarter to one-half an inch of water all the time. This 1020 greenhouse tray is perfect.

Containers with drainage sitting on a decorative plate that can hold water are a great way to show off your collection. JOHN BRUEGGEN

such as a 1020 greenhouse tray. These undrained seed flats can hold several pots. They can be found at local garden centers for around a dollar each. Plastic trays or children's pools with drainage are also ideal. Do not purchase clay saucers. Plastic cement mixer tubs are good too, but they are often too deep. When I have used them in the past, I drilled a hole about a half inch from the bottom. When the tray or container goes dry, but the plant's soil is still moist, refill the tray. This is also great for kids getting into gardening. When you send them out to water the plants, if they fill the tray too high, the drainage hole will automatically adjust the water level. Most carnivorous plants do not require overhead watering. Refilling the tray mimics the natural ebb and flow the plants experience in a bog.

As you turned to this page, I can only assume your eye jumped straight to the doll-head planters. This idea was inspired when I saw stores carrying plastic dinosaurs modified into

Happy customer with *Drosera spatulata* in custom baby head doll. DELPHINE GERACI

flowerpots. And before you imagine awful scenarios, I want to assure you that when I am summoned by the cashier at the thrift store, I always explain that I only need the heads of the dolls. I am sure this relieves them of their trepid thoughts.

The hard plastic these dolls are made of lasts for years—even in Florida's sun. And it's a quick and enjoyable DIY project. My father first drills a hole in the head to use the tin snips successfully. A small piece of screen, mesh plastic canvas, or similar is then added to keep the substrate in. Even though the heads appear small, their volume is close to or exceeds that of a three-inch pot, which is perfect for the life span of most Florida sundews and adequate for two or three years for young *Dionaea* and *Sarracenia*. Pro tip—if the doll's eyes roll back, superglue one down to give the appearance that it is winking at you. Keep the algae, peat debris, and soil on the face—it adds character. Around Halloween I cannot keep these in stock.

My dad showing off his handy work.

Growing your carnivorous plants in a backyard bog allows you to mix and match species to create a Florida-friendly focal point. Building a tiny ecosystem in a pot or bathtub or in a large man-made pool in your backyard allows you to admire the seasonal changes your plants experience and the wildlife they attract. Planning the species and designing the bog should be as much fun as watching it age over the years. A Master Gardener once asked me, "Do I plan a garden or plant one?" At the time I brazenly, and wrongly, replied, "Plant a garden." Now that I have many years of necessary transplanting behind me, I am painfully aware of how important it is to plan a garden first.

For a tabletop or pot-sized bog garden that's going to sit on your back deck, use approximately half peat moss and half perlite. Perlite keeps the soil loose and improves aeration. Perlite is favored over sand because of its light weight. I've also had problems with bags of sand containing salt and other mineral residue. Peat moss should be fertilizer-free, and you do not have to rinse it. Mix the peat moss and perlite together in a well-ventilated area since perlite will release dust. Be careful not to spill soil on the sundews, since this will make them unsightly for a month or more. Make sure the wet soil is compacted when plants

Mix and match carnivorous plant species in a large pot to add visual appeal. DELPHINE GERACI

are added. Use your hand to compress it in. If not, when it rains air holes will cause problems. Decorate as you please with logs, rocks, geodes, fairies, figurines, and dinosaurs. (When I host make-and-take bog, container, or terrarium classes, the delicate Master Gardener women are always first to take the dinosaur figurines, bypassing the fairies.) You can purchase plants for your bog garden, or you can divide from your existing plants. The beauty of a flush of *Utricularia* blooms should not be underestimated. Surrounding extra-large pots with flagstone helps hide the unsightly tub and bring focus to the carnivorous plants.

Another way to display your carnivorous plants is by drilling holes in porous rocks like pumice or lava rock. Firmly pack your standard carnivorous plant soil (see SOIL section) into the hole and transplant like you would in a regular pot. Adding a layer of live sphagnum moss will allow the display to theatrically age, as the moss moves into new nooks. In central Florida I have done okay with keeping sphagnum moss alive year-round. It does not enjoy the direct sun in the summer. These large rock containers can be placed in a saucer, as mentioned above, or put into grander displays.

Upcycling a clawfoot or free-standing tub makes for another unique carnivorous centerpiece for your backyard. If you're lucky enough to get one for your yard, you have a few options of how to display your plants. It is recommended that you place the tub on a platform or concrete pad, as it will sink into Florida's sandy native soils. One option for the tub is to make it a water rock garden. Purchase a rubber plug, and use silicone to secure it in place. After application, allow it to cure for twenty-four hours. The drain located near the top of the tub will ensure it maintains a suitable water level during the rainy season. To prop up your rock display so rocks are at their

Sarracenia species do well in a pond with or without fish. Create ledges in artificial ponds so that the water level is a quarter to halfway up the pot. SARRACENIA NORTHWEST

optimal height, place inverted nursery pots and trays or other nonbiodegradable objects that can support the rocks in the tub first. Then place the rocks in a manner that is appealing to you, keeping in mind the different species' light preferences. Use stones and rocks to stabilize your larger display pieces. Fill your tub with pure water, and enjoy the floating oasis. As the sphagnum grows and the species spread, your mini ecosystem will surely impress visitors and attract wildlife. Another option is to place potted plants in the tub or water feature. Provide enough infrastructure so that the water level is a quarter to halfway up the pot. Six-inch or larger pots are ideal.

A third use of the tub is to create a more standard bog. Sarracenia Northwest, a carnivorous plant nursery in Oregon, recommends that you create a reservoir of water using a PVC coupler over the tub's drain. Place a screen over the coupler and any other holes to keep the soil in. Fill the bottom with a layer of perlite. For this large container, use equal parts peat moss and perlite to encourage draining of excess moisture. Position your plants on top of the soil to make sure you are happy with their position and then transplant them. To prevent soil erosion, top-dress with a thin layer of pea gravel or coconut chips. This is ideal for a tub with large specimens like *Sarracenia*. The negative aspect of using a top dressing is that it will be harder for small species like Venus flytraps and *Drosera* to propagate through seed.

Mixing different container styles will add a lot of appeal to your landscape. SARRACENIA NORTHWEST

There are many options for those wanting to build a backyard bog directly in the ground. A large plastic tub or children's wading pool placed into a predug hole is an inexpensive option. I once purchased a kiddie pool from Toys "R" Us for ninety-seven cents. Did they go out of business shortly after? Yes, but that's a different story.

Children's wading pools come in different sizes, and I recommend the bigger the better. Your plants will divide, and you will run out of room quickly. Using a pond liner is another option, ideal for large installations. Dig a one-foot-deep hole, and place a pond liner down so it contours with the earth. Kidney-shaped or curved bogs are more aesthetically pleasing than squares. Leave at least a foot of the pond liner sticking out of the depression to accommodate settling. After establishing the bog with the soil and plants, you can cover the exposed pond liner with mulch, pebbles, or

Sarracenia leucophylla 'Hurricane Creek' in a bathtub bog. SARRACENIA NORTHWEST

flagstone. Whatever container you choose, drill a few tiny drainage holes or slits in it. Although you want your artificial bog to be saturated like a wrung-out sponge, allowing a slow flow of water through it during heavy rains is ideal. Fill the bog with equal parts peat moss and perlite or 30 to 50 percent coarse sand and the rest peat moss. After watering the bog thoroughly, wait a few hours or days before planting. When peat moss is dry, it is **hydrophobic**. Once the soil is saturated, you may begin planting. Bogs, opposed to backyard ponds, are good options for households with small children. Bogs also attract a variety of native animals, including amphibians, reptiles, and insects such as dragonflies, damselflies, and thirsty bees and butterflies.

Consider Adding These Noncarnivorous Native Florida Plants to Your Backyard Bog

Common Name	Botanical Name
Alligator flag (fire flag)	*Thalia geniculata*
Arrowhead	*Sagittaria* spp.
Blue flag iris	*Iris virginica*
Blueflower eryngo (marsh eryngo or rattlesnake master)	*Eryngium aquaticum*
Cardinal flower	*Lobelia cardinalis*
Horsetail	*Equisetum hyemal*
Lizard's tail	*Saururus cernuus*
Pickerel weed	*Pontederia lanceolata*
Rain lily	*Zephyranthes atamasco*
Scarlet hibiscus	*Hibiscus coccineus*
Spider lily	*Hymenocallis latifolia*
String lily	*Crinum americanum*

When designing your bog, use nature as your inspiration. Do not put the plants in a neat line. Grow them in groups or clumps. Taller plants should be planted in the northern region of the bog so they do not block sunlight for the shorter specimens. The bog should be supplementally watered when the soil begins to dry. Trim back dead foliage as you would for potted plants.

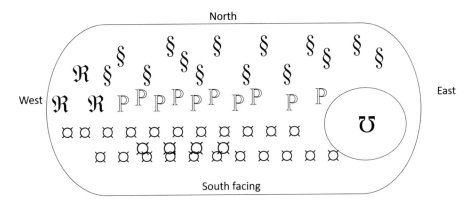

§	Tall varieties of *Sarracenia*
ℜ	*S. rosea*
ℙ	*Pinguicula*
¤	*Dionaea, Drosera, S. psittacina*, terrestrial *Utricularia*
℧	Aquatic *Utricularia* pool

Use this template as a model for your artificial bog. Consider sunlight and group plants together.

FERTILIZERS

When I first began growing carnivorous plants, I recommended against the use of fertilizers. When used as directed on the label, most are too strong for carnivorous plants. In the past decade, I have recommended a seaweed-based fertilizer called MaxSea. I have used it, but not systematically. My intention was to spray the plants every two weeks during their growing period. But with faulty computer calendars and general forgetfulness, many weeks went by between sprays. Some growers have a great affinity for MaxSea, while others doubt its effectiveness, as many books suggest using it at a quarter strength to not burn the plant. If you want your plants to grow healthy and strong, give them proper light. If you want to use fertilizers, I recommend creating a one-inch bath of MaxSea (half a teaspoon per gallon) and soaking your plants in the solution for ten minutes every two weeks. When you use a spray pump, it is difficult to gauge how much each plant is receiving. Better yet, place half of your carnivorous plants in the fertilizer and let the others grow naturally and see for yourself if it makes a difference.

Remember to check fertilizer bans if you live in Florida. Nearly one hundred communities place restrictions on using fertilizers containing phosphorous and nitrogen from June 1 through September 30. In addition to this period, it is also advised (and most likely the law depending on where you live) not to use fertilizers any time the National Weather Service forecasts heavy rains to occur within twenty-four hours. This regulation is intended for fertilizers used on your lawn and landscape. Sometimes I am able to purchase MaxSea (and other fertilizers) online, and other times I get a message saying it is restricted in my state. These pop-ups are unrelated to the time of year. MaxSea comes in a small container and would clearly not be for my landscape, much less my lawn.

The reason for the fertilizer bans is to prevent algae blooms caused by Florida's heavy rainstorms, which carry the excess nutrients from the ground to the local waterways. While red tide is a naturally occurring phenomenon, the situation is exacerbated when the algae is fed excess nutrients from fertilizers, sewage, livestock, and pet waste. While fish are most affected by red tide, invertebrates, sea turtles, sea birds, and marine mammals can also be contaminated with the toxins. If you fertilize, fertilize responsibly.

DORMANCY

It is normal for many of the Florida species to look rough starting in the late fall. The decrease in sunlight will cause them to start going into dormancy. If you have them on a windowsill, exposed to outdoor photoperiods, they will start to go dormant regardless of your house temperature. Expect *Sarracenia*, Venus flytraps, and *Drosera* to be in their dormant stages from Thanksgiving to Valentine's Day. *Sarracenia* pitchers will begin to brown from the top, going all the way down to the rhizome. You can cut them off as you want or, better yet, give the *Sarracenia* a buzz cut in January. If you miss it and new growth starts to emerge, cut the dried pitchers individually, leaving the new growth.

Different species go into dormancy at different times. For example, *Sarracenia flava* goes dormant sooner. *Sarracenia leucophylla* goes dormant later in the season. *Sarracenia flava* emerges earlier in the spring, so mixed plantings would be a good idea in a bog garden or collection.

A Venus flytrap's tall summer traps will blacken and die back to the rhizome, producing a lower rosette of traps as they enter dormancy. Sundews produce a dormant bud called a hibernaculum. All the Florida *Pinguicula* species

This *Sarracenia rubra* subsp. *gulfensis* isn't dead; it's dormant!

are winter growers, looking their best in January and February just before blooming. In late summer they are at their worst, as they do not like high temperatures.

If you live in the northern part of the state, you are lucky in that you will not need to do anything extra for your plant's dormancy period. Leave them outside and they will do great, as they are native to the region. In central Florida I leave North American species out year-round. If there are freezing temperatures for a couple of days, it's fine—they'll enjoy the rest. For my Asian pitcher plants, I protect the highland *Nepenthes* with the shelter of the greenhouse or pool house if the temperature is going to fall below 45°F and the lowland *Nepenthes* when it falls below 70°F.

LIGHT

The majority of Florida's carnivorous plants do best in direct sunlight. They are found in open bogs and savannas with little to no tree coverage. Keep this in mind when choosing a location for a bog or potted plants. For a few years, I grew all carnivorous plants in the pool lanai or greenhouse. The area around the pool received full sun in the morning and was in shade by the late afternoon. After experimenting with the metal roof of the chicken coop, I now grow all the retail *Sarracenia* there (several hundred). The chicken coop, pool, and vegetable garden are the only areas that receive adequate sunlight throughout the day. The rest of the property has oak trees scattered about, and although I love carnivorous plants, I could not fathom cutting down the ancient trees to get more sun in the yard, as some solar panel experts have suggested. So with my limited sun, all *Sarracenia* grow on the chicken coop roof, with the exception of *Sarracenia rosea* and my personal collection of fifteen *Sarracenia* plants. They remain in the sunniest part of the pool lanai, so I can enjoy them as I float about. The plants on the roof, growing in the tray method, grow faster and more robust with the extra three hours of sunlight. They still are protected from the late western sun but are now exposed to the morning sun earlier. My personal collection of *Nepenthes*, *Drosera*, cacti, and succulents grow in the greenhouse with terrestrial and aquatic *Utricularia*, *Pinguicula*, and *Dionaea* growing in the pool lanai.

Tropical plants like *Nepenthes* and some sundews and butterworts do not require a dormancy period. These plants are from tropical locations where they enjoy heat and sun year-round. If you choose to grow these inside, provide twelve to fourteen hours of light year-round and warm temperatures to keep them happy. There are a variety of grow lights available and many websites dedicated to the subject. I only have experience growing *Nepenthes* in a south-facing window without the use of supplemental lighting.

PESTS

Yes, the tables can turn and bugs can end up eating your carnivorous plants. Overall, I have had great success in keeping most species of carnivorous plants healthy. My biggest pest problems include cut worms, thrips, mealybug, and scale. Slugs and snails are usually so large I'm able to remove them and feed them to the chicken flock before they do much damage. Since most of my plants are grown in a screened-in lanai or on top of the chicken coop six feet above the ground, I do not experience raccoon, opossum, or squirrel problems. Once I had a beautiful six-foot vine of *Nepenthes* hanging from a tree. The next day I saw a squirrel ripping open the pitchers to eat the *Nepenthes'* meal. After that the *Nepenthes* collection moved permanently inside the pool lanai and greenhouse.

Cutworms have sporadically predated on my *Sarracenia*, *Pinguicula*, and *Nepenthes*. They have ignored my Venus flytraps and *Drosera*. Cutworms can be found at night with a flashlight. Trickier pests to get rid of include mealybug, scale,

A smartweed caterpillar (*Acronicta oblinita*) dines on the carnivorous *Sarracenia flava*.
BILL MCLAUGHLIN

Occasionally the prey can chew themselves to freedom.

and thrips. While I could use pesticides, I find it just as easy to cut off the infected pitchers and dispose of them properly. This sometimes means composting them on site if the compost is active and hot. More often I throw the contaminated leaves in the yard waste bin. Most infestations occur during the winter. They can also occur when plants are not given enough sunlight. Scale and thrips can be scraped off and killed by insecticides. Do not use soap or aerosol insecticides. Wettable insecticidal powders, Orthene or Bifenthrin, are recommended.

SOIL

Earlier I mentioned half peat moss and half perlite as a suitable option for a bog garden. Many plants that people start growing in their carnivorous collection also do well in a combination of washed play sand and sphagnum peat moss. Both are available at home improvement stores and plant nurseries. Your carnivorous plants will not survive if given regular potting soil. Long-fiber sphagnum and live sphagnum moss are also suitable options. I have played around with proportions of all of these and have had good success. Many times for me it is about price, as I resell many of these plants and want to keep the prices competitive. If I am going to keep the plant, I use 100 percent long-fiber sphagnum for my Asian *Nepenthes* and half and half play sand and peat moss for my North American carnivorous plants. But I've also used 100 percent long-fiber sphagnum for North American plants.

WATER

Carnivorous plants love water—specifically pure water. Water is the most important thing you can give your plant. Over seventy million years, carnivorous plants have evolved to live in nutrient-poor soils. They get around this obstacle by eating prey. The same is true of their relationship to water. They have evolved to live in wet areas that contain little to no nutrients. Water that contains salts and minerals will build up in your pots and quickly kill your plant. This means tap and hose water is generally *not* acceptable.

Collecting rainwater is a free option. To water my one thousand carnivorous plants, I have five fifty-gallon rain barrels. They quickly fill up in a heavy storm. I then use the water as needed, with the seasonal rain refilling my source. The interesting phenomenon about growing carnivorous plants in central Florida is that during the rainy season (late May through mid-October) my rain barrels are full, and I don't often have to supplement the plants with water because it is always raining. As the temperature cools, there is less evaporation in my trays, and I do not use a lot of water. In the springtime, after the prolonged dry spell,

Filling one-gallon jugs from your rain barrel to get you through the dry season is a wonderful tip that I learned from my neighbor Demi Stearns. Florida's rain patterns are very much feast or famine.

and as the mercury rises, I occasionally get lucky and use the last drop of the fifth barrel before a good rainstorm replenishes all of them. But one year I did not make it through the dry season. And due to Covid-19, all the stores were in short supply of jugs of water. So that year I could be seen at the local retention pond, filling up twelve one-gallon jugs every morning until it rained again. After that traumatic experience, I now fill one-gallon water, juice, and milk jugs from my rain barrels during the rainy season to be prepared. I could simply add another fifty-gallon rain barrel, but I am running out of downspouts and this is an easy solution.

If you care for a few carnivorous plants, purchasing distilled water from a grocery store is relatively cheap. Gallons sell for one dollar or less. Bottled distilled water and bottled spring water are not the same. Distilled water is made by collecting the steam of boiled water, while spring water may contain nitrates and metals. Purchasing purified water, "now with vitamins and minerals added" is also counterproductive. Filters on your faucet (like Brita®) are usually not good enough for carnivorous plants.

If you have a larger collection of carnivorous plants and collecting rainwater or purchasing bottled water is not economical, installing a reverse osmosis system is a straightforward option. Those who have delicate aquarium systems or are overly concerned about their health will most likely be familiar with this system of filtration. When purchasing, look for one that produces 50 parts per million (ppm) or lower TDS (total dissolved solids). Venus flytraps and *Pinguicula* do best with 0 ppm. Other carnivorous plants would do okay with 50–140 ppm, especially *Nepenthes* that are in hanging baskets. Remember, the lower the number, the purer the water. If you use water with more than 0 ppm, those contaminants will build up in your soil, which will require you to transplant into fresh soil more frequently. Reverse osmosis systems will run a few hundred dollars. The rainwater I collect from my metal roof is 0 ppm, the hose water is around 50 ppm, and the tap water is 300 ppm, to give you an idea. But depending on where you live, your water municipalities, and the current systems, you might be able to use what you already have. A twenty-dollar TDS meter (ppm pen) will conveniently keep you updated on your water quality. When purchasing a reverse osmosis system, research the wastewater ratio. The reverse osmosis system will produce two streams at the end of the purifying process. One will be the filtered water and the other will be wastewater, which contains sediments and minerals. Collect the wastewater and reuse it for landscape plants or to wash your car. Knowing the waste-to-product ratio will keep you informed on how efficient the system is.

Sitting a bucket of water out for twenty-four hours *might* help with an aquarium, as the chlorine evaporates, but this system is ineffective for carnivorous plants. The minerals, metals, and other contaminants will still be there the next day—possibly in higher concentrations since some of the water will have evaporated.

CARNIVOROUS PLANTS AS INSECTICIDES

Although Darwin titled his book *Insectivorous Plants*, we know now that these carnivorous plants prey outside of the huge class Insecta and even outside of the phylum Arthroropoda. *Dionaea*, for example, eat members of the Mollusca phylum, and *Sarracenia* eat earthworms, spiders, and woodlice. *Utricularia* digest fish and tadpoles. But, in general, these plants have adapted and refined their mechanisms to dieting on arthropods. The other creatures are a culinary bonus.

While carnivorous plants are beautiful and amazing due to their shapes and characteristics, it's also villainous to think about all the buggy snacks you'll feed them. Just a small caution: these plants will not be able to eliminate all your pests. Though some carnivorous plants are generalists and eat a variety of bugs, many lure and trap specific bugs. Most carnivorous plants produce sweet nectar that attracts flies, wasps, and moths. Unless by accident, those plants are not going to catch a mosquito. If you have pots sitting in stagnant water, you may find your backyard actually attracting more mosquitoes.

Carnivorous plants in Florida eat a range of organisms, including rotifers, water fleas, moths, wasps, ants, and occasionally small frogs and lizards. PHOTOS BY CREATIVE COMMONS

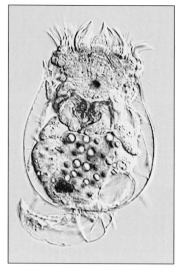

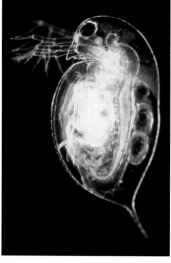

Brachionus calyciflorus is a freshwater species of rotifer.

Daphnia pulex is a common species of water flea.

Araneus pegnia is a species of orb weaver.

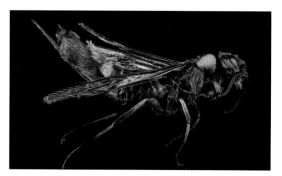

Eriotremex formosanus. Asian horntail.

Polistes are a common group of paper wasps in North America.

Vespula are also known as yellowjackets.

Solenopsis molesta are known as thief ants.

Venus Flytraps

Just like me and so many other Florida residents, Venus flytraps are transplants. Although not endemic to Florida, Venus flytraps are highlighted in this book because they are *the* carnivorous plant. Also, they are now growing in Florida and have been doing so for at least fifty years. Although theories include former sellers planting "three bulbs for a dollar" flytraps as a backup reservoir to seed migrating down on birds, a carnivorous plant collector did admit recently to broadcasting seed in 1973 or 1974 near Hosford bog, in Liberty County, which could account for the **allochthonous** populations still seen today.

Venus flytraps are native to the acidic wetlands of a small region in North and South Carolina. Their native habitat is hot and wet in the summer and cooler and drier in the winter. To grow Venus flytraps successfully, you should replicate their natural habitat. This includes duplicating their soil conditions, amount of sunlight, water quality and quantity, and of course the most fun part—their diet.

Venus flytraps attract their prey based on their traps mimicking the scent of insect food. Insects that wander into the hinged lobes are trapped in the plant's teeth, which act like prison bars. Each lobe has two to four trigger hairs. Once a trigger hair is touched, an electrical signal is sent to the other lobe. The Venus flytrap then starts counting. In 2016, a team led by biophysicist Rainer Hedrich, a professor at Julius-Maximilians-Universität Würzburg in Bavaria, Germany, proved that Venus flytraps can count to five. In 2019, the scientists won a research prize worth 1.5 million euros to find out how Venus flytraps count.

When a trigger hair is touched, an explosion of electrical activity is created. This is called an action potential. The electrical signal spreads throughout the entire trap. (Each plant has four to twenty traps at one time.) This electrical information is translated into a chemical calcium wave. One touch of the trigger hair does not make the wave of energy large enough for the trap to close. If the trigger hair is touched again within

A few of the allochthonous Venus flytraps growing in Florida's panhandle. ALEX ROUKIS

A covey of carnivorous flytraps. FLORENT CHOUFFOT

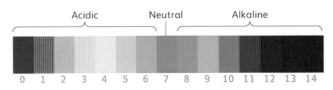

pH is a measure of how many hydrogen ions there are in a solution. Acids are a chemical that have a lot of hydrogen ions. When mixed with water, they release one of its protons. Bases accept protons when mixed with water. Potenz is German for power and H represents the periodic symbol hydrogen. That is why we call it pH.

twenty to thirty seconds, the action potential electrically excites the trap and the lobes snap shut. If the insect doesn't trigger the hair a second time, it is able to escape.

When the trigger hairs are prompted more than twice, the plant hormone jasmonate is increased. From the fifth action potential on, the Venus flytrap produces digestive enzymes to break down the prey and transport proteins to aid in the absorption of the nutrients. This is good to know because if you feed your Venus flytrap pre-killed prey and place it in the trap, the trap may reopen after an hour since there is no struggling motion to prompt the production of enzymes. It is therefore recommended that you gently massage prekilled prey, like bloodworms, in the traps for a little while to mimic a struggling insect.

Scientists believe that the Venus flytrap evolved to wait for the second trigger so that it wouldn't waste energy by accidently closing due to wind or rain. When the lobes are triggered, the traps close in about one hundred milliseconds, going from convex to concave. The teeth interlock to form a cage. The more the victim struggles, the tighter the lobes shut. After an hour or so, the trap is locked completely. Now the cells of the edges of the lobes produce digestive

Native to the Carolinas, Florida's rogue population of Venus flytraps have been doing well in the panhandle for at least fifty years. JIM FOWLER

enzymes like those of your stomach. Depending on the size of the prey, it takes four to ten days for prey to be digested. When the trap is done eating the meal, the lobes open, revealing the prey's exoskeleton. Wind, rain, or another bug eventually remove the exoskeleton, and the snare is ready to trap again. Any trap that is open is ready to eat.

Healthy plants can handle you setting off their traps occasionally. It's fun to watch a plant react. Watching them move will help you know if your plant is healthy. If the plant's lobes close slowly, the traps are either old or the plant is not getting enough light.

Venus flytraps live in sunny pocosins. Depending on where you live, the easiest way to grow a healthy Venus flytrap is probably to grow it outside in a very sunny location. It will grow faster in warmer weather and slow down and hibernate when it gets cool. In the wild they survive winters that get slightly below freezing.

Don't worry—this Florida box turtle (*Terrapene carolina bauri*) hatchling is not on the menu. JOHN BRUEGGEN

If you want to display your Venus flytrap in a terrarium with a grow light, you can catch live spiders and flies and release them into the terrarium. Most terrariums are not ideal or necessary for carnivorous plants. If you keep your plant outdoors, it will attract and trap its own meals.

When I asked Maggie Chen of California how she gets her award-winning Venus flytrap so big, her secret made me laugh out loud.

"I put my dogs' waste can under the tables," she told me. The odor attracts the plants' next meal. She added that she uses really tall pots to shield them from high heat and repots the plants every six to nine months to make sure mineral residues don't build up. She says that pure long-fiber sphagnum moss makes them grow faster since it is less compact and provides more aeration.

If you want to grow a Venus flytrap indoors on a windowsill or in your room, you will need to provide it with artificial light. Light coming from a window is simply not enough. For one plant, find a twenty-five-watt bulb that has fifteen thousand to twenty-five thousand lux of white LED lighting. The light should be kept on for fourteen hours a day, year-round. If you have your plant set up in these conditions, it will not go dormant and will grow continually. It will require regular meals, so feed it often to encourage new growth.

Maggie Chen's *Dionaea* 'Red Dentate' won second place in the Bay Area Carnivorous Plant Society 2020 virtual show. Its traps grow up to two inches, and this is her favorite red variety for its vigor and size. MAGGIE CHEN

Charles Darwin was among the first to publish evidence that plants have the ability to capture and digest insects in his 1875 book *Insectivorous Plants*. In his book he wrote that Venus flytraps are "the most wonderful plant in the world."

Venus flytraps are indeed wonderful. Sadly, their conservation status is "vulnerable" to extinction. Their native Carolina wetlands are being turned into suitable land for lumber and agriculture. Governments and city developers drain the wetlands to build houses for the exponential growth of the human population. People also stop naturally occurring brushfires caused by lightning. When naturally occurring brushfires are prevented, bushes and trees continue to grow and block out sunlight that the Venus flytraps need. Decades ago, people would steal large amounts of plants from the Carolinas to sell them. Today, this is less of a problem due to the ease of growing them under human care. Collectors also now favor fanciful cultivated varieties, which have wacky traps, grow extra small or large, or have different colors than the typical wild type. The other reason that poaching is not that big of a problem is sadly that there isn't enough to poach. If poachers are caught stealing plants from the wild, they are fined and possibly sent to prison.

In Florida's panhandle we have a rogue population. Many don't consider them invasive since the population hasn't spread. To be considered invasive, they must be able to establish on many sites, grow fast, and

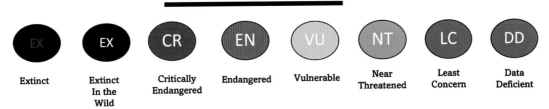

The conservation status indicates if the group still exists and how likely they are to become extinct in the near future.

propagate to the point of disturbing other plant communities or ecosystems. A more appropriate term for the rogue colonies of Venus flytraps would be *naturalized*. Naturalization is when a non-native species spreads into the ecosystem and its reproduction is adequate to sustain its population. Since the Venus flytraps have been here for fifty years, they fit the description. While it is not appropriate to plant more Venus flytraps in the wilds of Florida, it also doesn't seem right to dig them up, which you'll see signs of.

When showing off your Venus flytraps to your friends, share the history of this amazing plant. Teach them about conserving plants. Plants are typically at the bottom of the food chain, which makes this snappy predator a highly desired household companion.

Flowers of *Dionaea muscipula* in Liberty County, Florida.
MANNY HERRERA

Dionaea muscipula in Liberty County, Florida.   PHOTOS BY MANNY HERRERA

34

FEEDING YOUR VENUS FLYTRAP

If kept outside, Venus flytraps will find their own meal. If indoors, catch insects in a jar and slow the bugs down by placing them in the fridge. After they have slowed down, place them in a trap. If you can't catch a fly or it is the wrong season, purchase dried bloodworms from a pet store. Rehydrate a large pinch of worms in distilled water. Place them in the trap, then massage the trap to replicate the desperate motion of prey. If you don't, the traps will reopen hours later thinking it was a pebble or dirt. They need to feel the struggle!

Commonly cared-for carnivores. Look for these to add to your collection.

Venus flytrap 'Akai Ryu'.

Venus flytrap 'CCCP Red Onyx'. CCCP CRAZY CRAIG'S CARNIVOROUS PLANTS

Venus flytrap 'Ginormous'. DAVID THURBON

Venus flytrap 'Red Burgundy'. MAGGIE CHEN

Venus flytrap 'Big Tomato'. MAGGIE CHEN

Venus flytrap 'Kim Jong Un'. MAGGIE CHEN

Venus flytrap 'Bloody Nurse'. MAGGIE CHEN

Venus flytrap 'Predator'. MAGGIE CHEN

Venus flytrap 'St. Patrick's Beard'. MAGGIE CHEN

Venus flytrap 'Cross Teeth'. FLORENT CHOUFFOT

Venus flytrap 'Shark Teeth'. FLORENT CHOUFFOT

37

Venus flytrap 'Sawtooth'. FLORENT CHOUFFOT

Venus flytrap 'Fused Tooth Alien'. MAGGIE CHEN

North American Pitcher Plants

Sarracenia minor was first described in a manuscript back in 1576. Many years later, in the early 1700s, Canadian scientist Michel Sarrazin sent a pitcher plant to France to be described. Linnaeus called the genus *Sarracenia* to honor Sarrazin and made it official in a publication in 1753. In the 1870s and 1880s, something amazing happened—people realized these plants ate bugs. Yes, it took the public over three hundred years to understand and accept the fact that a plant could not only kill but benefit from eating bugs. It was North Carolinian doctor Joseph Hinson Mellichamp who investigated *Sarracenia* and proved they are carnivorous. Dr. Mellichamp published the first experiment that showed carnivory in *any* plant, although other scientists had similar ideas. Sarrazin, on the contrary, noticed the dead bugs floating inside the pitcher plant's leaves but didn't think they were providing nutrients to the plant.

Sarracenia species and hybrids are stunning plants that are often first to sell at my table at plant sales around the state. For a long time, I told audiences at plant shows and presentations that they were my favorite. The extensive research needed for this book has enlightened me and renewed my interest in all the wonders that each genus provides. It is too difficult now to have a true favorite. But a three-foot towering pitcher is a hard plant to dismiss.

Sarracenia elegance has been celebrated since the early nineteenth century, when people valued them for their ornamental properties. Artificial hybrids were made in England through the Veitch Nurseries as early as 1906. The Veitch Nurseries were the largest group of family-run plant nurseries in Europe during the Victorian era. The dynasty had over twenty plant hunters who collected around the world and introduced over one thousand plants into cultivation, including the carnivorous pitcher plant *Nepenthes* from Asia.

Today, species and complex hybrids of *Sarracenia* are commonly available to hobbyists and displayed at botanical gardens. Tissue cultures of some hybrids are so widely available that they cost less than a dollar for a **plug**.

Sarracenia are sexy. Not only do they reproduce within the same species; they also readily hybridize. This unusual phenomenon of producing fertile crosses that can further hybridize makes for some beautiful cultivars. Along the Gulf Coast, hybrid swarms of *Sarracenia* crosses ranging in genetic and **phenotypic** qualities are famous. This makes them a bit difficult to identify in the wild.

Sarracenia rosea. BILL MCLAUGHLIN

Sarracenia ×naczii petals begin yellow-flushed pink and age to rich rose-pink. BILL MCLAUGHLIN

Naturally Occurring Hybrids Found in Florida

Nothospecies	Cross
×bellii	*Sarracenia leucophylla* × *Sarracenia rubra* subsp. *gulfensis*
×chelsonii	*Sarracenia purpurea* × *Sarracenia rubra*
×courtii	*Sarracenia psittacina* × *Sarracenia purpurea*
×gilpinii	*Sarracenia pstitticina* × *Sarracenia rubra*
×harperi	*Sarracenia flava* × *Sarracenia minor*
×mitchelliana	*Sarracenia leucophylla* × *Sarracenia purpurea*
×moorei	*Sarracenia flava* × *Sarracenia leucophylla*
×naczii	*Sarracenia flava* × *Sarracenia rosea*
×readei	*Sarracenia leucophylla* × *Sarracenia rubra*
×wrigleyana	*Sarracenia leucophylla* × *Sarracenia psittacina*

To identify *Sarracenia*, look for subtle pitcher leaf traits and pay less attention to flower characteristics. To properly identify a species, large samples of mature pitchers growing in ideal conditions must be studied. Pitchers from dry soil or heavily shaded areas will not display the plants' ideal characteristics. The dichotomous key at the end of the chapter is based on an archetype.

Anthocyanins are water-soluble vacuolar pigments that cause plants to appear red, purple, blue, or black. In the wild, most species of *Sarracenia* have been found as an anthocyanin-free form. This results in an all-green plant, including the flowers and pitchers. As these are highly collectible, poachers have been known to collect entire populations. Typical pitcher plants range in cost from five to twenty dollars, whereas a single anthocyanin-free plant can sell for one hundred dollars. Complex, robust, colorful hybrids can fetch similar prices. Ethical nurseries and breeders know how to properly collect seed or take nondisruptive root cuttings and propagate them vegetatively for everyone to enjoy. Legally, this would only occur on private property where the breeder has permission.

The modified leaves of *Sarracenia* form conical pitchers that trap many insects, including pollinators, for supplemental nutrition. The traps of *Sarracenia* can be divided into zones. The zones help the plant lure, trap, or digest its prey.

An anthocyanin-free *Sarracenia rosea*.

A typical form of *Sarracenia rosea*.
VICTOR A. ALBERT

Lids serve as landing pods for a variety of insects. JOHN BRUEGGEN

- Zone 1 (Attraction): *Operculumin* in Latin means "cover or lid." However, these lids do not close. They serve more as an attractive landing pad for flying insects. The scent and colors attract bugs to the trap. The operculum, for most species, prevents excess rain from going into the pitcher. This prevents the digestive fluids from becoming diluted. On the underside of the operculum are downward-facing hairs. These hairs help guide the victim to the next zone.

- Zone 2 (Conduction): The peristome produces attractive nectar to position the bugs just right. The waxy upper part of the pitcher is very slippery. This is where the bugs lose their grip while drinking the nectar.
- Zone 3 (Glandular): This next zone has some more downward-facing hairs that cause the insects to fall deeper into the trap as they cannot get a foothold. If they are able to manage the smooth leaf surface, the hairs would be uncomfortable and poke them back down. This area is covered with digestive glands that drip enzymes into the fluid below. If a flying insect is caught, the tubes are usually too narrow for it to open its wings and escape.
- Zone 4 (Digestion/Absorption): The last part of the trap is the digestive fluid. It has a wetting agent that causes wings and legs not to work. After the insect drowns, the fluid and bacteria break down the meal into digestible parts. Some *Sarracenia* species have commensals living in the liquid that eat the drowned prey, thus helping the pitcher plant benefit from the smaller pieces.
- Zone 5 (Unknown Zone): Only found (or visible) in *Sarracenia rosea* and *Sarracenia purpurea*, this extra zone is a small reddish addition at the base of the pitcher. It lacks hairs and glands. This zone's function is still unknown.

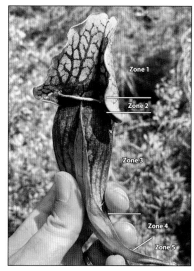

Sarracenia rosea with zones labeled.
VICTOR A. ALBERT

In my TED-Ed Talk, I wrote that the nectar of one species of pitcher plant (*Sarracenia flava*) includes an ingredient called coniine (sadly misspelled in the video). This chemical is a powerful narcotic to insects. Coniine is also found in poison hemlock, which is toxic to humans and livestock. As the coniine takes effect on the pitcher's prey, the prey become sluggish and basically intoxicated. Scientists still do not know where the coniine is biosynthesized, since the compound has been detected both in the lids and in the actual pitchers. Coniine is classified as an alkaloid, which is a chemical compound that has at least one nitrogen atom. Scientists questioned why a plant living in a nutrient-poor environment (one that lacks nitrogen) would produce a nitrogenous compound if that is what they require to grow. In addition to the plant's coniine-laced nectar, which causes the bugs to become tipsy, the coniine could also attract insects as it has a floral scent. It appears that the plants are investing their nitrogen atoms for coniine biosynthesis in order to attract and trap insects, leading to more nitrogen. As of publication, scientists have discovered coniine in at least six additional *Sarracenia* species—although oftentimes in low concentrations.

Another trade-off carnivorous plants face is their relationship with insects, as insects serve as both pollinators and prey. One way carnivorous plants avoid eating their own pollinators is by carefully timing when the plant produces flowers and when it produces active traps. For *Sarracenia*, having highly distinct scent profiles in their flowers and pitchers allows those parts to target different species. This lessens the chance of accidentally eating their own pollinators—but it isn't foolproof.

Many *Sarracenia* begin the year by producing flowers prior to pitchers. Standing on one- to three-foot-tall stalks, depending on the species, the flowers hang loosely. Flowers are one to four inches in diameter and range from yellowish to shades of red. Their flowers are unique, and their complexity is reminiscent of an orchid. *Sarracenia* have highly modified pistils that resemble an upside-down umbrella. The pistil is the female part of the flower, which comprises a stigma, style, and ovary. The five tips of the umbrella are the stigmas. The stigma is the part that receives pollen and begins the process of fertilization. The five petals at the base of the bell-shaped flower are spread out, filling the space between the stigmas. This positions pollinators, which are often bees, to enter between the draping petals and over the stigma. Once inside, they buzz around. They pick up pollen that has fallen from the stamens and has conveniently collected on the floor of the inverted umbrella style. To exit, they push through the hanging petals, which reduces the chance of self-pollination. As they enter the next flower, they cross-pollinate by brushing against the stigma as they enter. The flowers' shape guides the bees' entrances and exits and improves the chance of cross-pollination, which in turn increases genetic variation, which helps plants to survive in changing environments. After about a week to ten days, the petals start to fall and the seeds begin to develop underneath the stigma. The huge stigma remains and is reminiscent of an angular clock face. In the past, people have called these plants dumb watches, as they have no numbers and no hands.

Sarracenia flowers span one to four inches in diameter and range from yellowish to shades of red. JOHN BRUEGGEN

As an avid admirer of sloths, I cannot help but notice the similarities between them and *Sarracenia*. Sloth fur can be home to a variety of arthropods, like moths, beetles, cockroaches, and even worms. In addition, there can be different trophic levels, like symbiotic fungi, cyanobacteria, and algae, which the arthropods interact with. The sloth fur ecosystem is within the larger rainforest ecosystem. Pitcher plants also host an elaborate food web of predators, prey, and detritivores. These organisms, like the sloths' **epibionts**, live in an ecosystem within an ecosystem. These trophic levels within trophic levels, stacked like Russian dolls, are mesmerizing. Huzzah!

While carnivorous pitcher plants do get the job done, they are not successful at killing all the organisms that enter the trap. Some species, ranging from bacteria to vertebrates, can not only survive but even reproduce inside the otherwise deadly pitcher. The **phytotelma** of *Sarracenia purpurea* has been studied more than any other carnivorous pitcher plant. It has been estimated that at least thirty species inhabit *Sarracenia purpurea*. Protozoa, algae, rotifers, spiders, caterpillars, and flies have all taken refuge in the carnivorous pitcher whose upturned hood welcomes rainwater. Species like *Sarracenia flava*, *Sarracenia leucophylla*, and *Sarracenia rubra*, whose habitats overlap that of *Sarracenia purpurea*, have much fewer species of **inquilines**. This could be due to hood shape, the pitcher's individual life span, or fluid quality.

Since most pitchers die in the late fall, a fun activity is to cut the pitchers vertically. This dissection allows you to see a column of creatures that the pitchers feasted on during the growing season. Warning: this activity isn't for the faint of heart. Sometimes dead, dried-up bugs sitting in digestive enzymes smell. But kids love it.

Florida currently lists five of the six native pitcher plant species as threatened or endangered. This is due to draining the wetlands for pine plantations and more likely urban sprawl and development. According to a 1982 study, less than 3 percent of the original habitat along the Gulf Coastal Plain remains for these plants. I'm afraid to find out the percentage left now, with close to one thousand people a day moving to Florida.

To help, we should promote and understand that frequent prescribed burning can help control hardwood species. This is a natural phenomenon that we should allow. It helps reveal necessary sunlight to the pitcher plants. Locations with disrupted hydrology should be restored, including those affected by feral hogs. Fencing and removing hogs will help mitigate past damages. With an estimated one million wild hogs in Florida, as a vegetarian, I see no problem with promoting "naturally raised," "free-range," and "local" porkchops in Florida restaurants. People released them here, and people need to fix the problem.

Poaching is always a problem with unique plants. Signs explaining the ecological niche of pitcher plants and their threatened status may help deter poaching in parks. Parkgoers need to be diligent about not posting photos with GPS coordinates that aid digitally competent poachers.

SARRACENIA ALABAMENSIS SUBSP. WHERRYI

Although *Sarracenia alabamensis* subsp. *wherryi* is primarily from Alabama, Florida has a small population in northwestern Escambia County. We do not have *Sarracenia alabamensis* subsp. *alabmensis* in Florida. The subspecies *wherryi*, compared to subspecies *alabamensis*, has much smaller pitchers and less dense clumps. The spring pitchers are delicate and thin, with the summer pitchers growing only twelve to sixteen inches tall with a red line down the front of the **ala**. The pitchers are dull green with bronze or red over-tones. This subspecies can be found in coastal plain habitats.

The original publication in 1974 by Case and Case detailing *Sarracenia alabamensis* and *Sarracenia alabamensis* subsp. *wherryi* was nullified due to a methodology error. Then in 1978, Schnell assigned both invalid names to subspecies *Sarracenia rubra*, which made an invalid name *Sarracenia rubra* subsp. *alabamensis* and the valid *Sarracenia rubra* subsp. *wherryi*. In 2005, Case corrected the error, which validated both *S. alabamensis* and *S. alabamensis* subsp. *wherryi*. See, isn't taxonomy fun!

Sarracenia alabamensis subsp. *wherryi*

Scientific name		*Sarracenia alabamensis* subsp. *wherryi*
Basionym/synonyms		*Sarracenia rubra* subsp. *wherryi*, Wherry's pitcher plant
Florida status		Threatened
Florida distribution		East of the Perdido River in northwestern Escambia County, Florida
United States range		Northern Mobile and southwestern Washington counties, Alabama, and in extreme eastern Greene and Wayne counties, Mississippi
Plant characteristics		Forms sparse clumps
Pitcher	Color	Dull green, often strongly suffused bronze or red
	Height	8–48 cm, average 18 cm tall
	Stature	Monomorphic, spring and summer pitchers erect
	Areolae	Absent
Phyllodia		Absent
Scapes		14–40 cm
Flower	Color	Crimson to maroon
	Blooming season	April
	Scent	Raspberries
Habitat		Boggy ditches, seeps, meadows, savannas, pine flatwoods
Elevation		20–90 m

SOURCE: EFLORAS.ORG

Sarracenia alabamensis subsp. *wherryi*.

Sarracenia alabamensis subsp. *wherryi*. BILL MCLAUGHLIN

SARRACENIA FLAVA

Pitcher colors of *Sarracenia flava* range from chartreuse to crimson to a stunning yellow with red veining. This range makes it the most variable *Sarracenia* species. In the panhandle, a variety known as *Sarracenia flava* var. *rugelii* has large, vigorous pitchers that are entirely green except for a red throat blotch. Hobbyists refer to it as "cutthroat." Nearby there are a few populations named *Sarracenia flava* var. *rubricorpora*, which have red pitchers and green lids with red veining. Each of these rhizomes puts out one or two pitchers in the spring, which are then followed by noncarnivorous phyllodia leaves that are also tinted red. They resemble swords. In the late summer, a couple more carnivorous pitchers may be produced. Even more rare in the wild, but extremely sought

Sarracenia flava flowers. BILL MCLAUGHLIN

after in cultivation, is the deep red variety *atropurpurea*. The variety *ornata* is a highly variable plant with yellow-green pitchers that have red-purple reticulated veining covering most of the pitcher. The more veins, the more expensive. Seeds that are self-pollinated that originate from the Florida Panhandle do not produce offspring that resemble the mother plant. Self-pollinated seeds from the variety of *rubricorpora* produce offspring when mature that resemble a mixture of var. *ornata*, var. *rugelli*, and var. *rubricorpora* and some that resemble a hybrid of all three. This is a testament to how promiscuous *Sarracenia* is. I recommend that you don't overanalyze them and instead appreciate and grow whatever pleases your eye, regardless of their parentage or name.

Sarracenia flava var. *rugelii*. Liberty County, Florida.
MANNY HERRERA

Sarracenia flava var. *ornata*. Liberty County, Florida. MANNY HERRERA

Sarracenia flava var. *rubricorpora*. Liberty County, Florida.
MANNY HERRERA

Sarracenia flava can grow to over three feet high. They specialize in wasps, hornets, flies, and bees and can be so gluttonous they tip over. Spiders will often spin a web at the entrance of the pitcher to steal meals. Their peristome is thickly rolled and resembles the spout of a pitcher. The lids act as large heliports for insects and are either entirely flat or flare upward at the edges. The drooping five yellow petals provide its name, *flava*, which in Latin means "yellow."

Sarracenia flava

Scientific name		*Sarracenia flava*
Synonyms		Yellow trumpet, yellow pitcher plant
Florida status		Least concern
Florida distribution		Bay, Calhoun, Escambia, Franklin, Gadsden, Gulf, Holmes, Jackson, Leon, Liberty, Okaloosa, Santa Rosa, Wakulla, Walton, Washington
United States range		*Sarracenia flava* can be found in the Atlantic and Gulf Coastal Plains of southeastern Virginia, North Carolina, South Carolina, Georgia, western Florida, and Alabama
Plant characteristics		Forms dense clumps
Pitcher	Color	Yellowish-green in color, with a reddish-purple blotch at the back of the opening
	Height	50–90 cm
	Stature	Erect and tubular
	Areolae	Absent
	Rim color	Green, flaring, and loosely **revolute**
Phyllodia		2–4, erect
Scapes		15–60 cm, shorter than pitchers
Flower	Color	Sepals yellowish-green, 3–5 cm × 2–3.5 cm; petals yellow
	Seed capsules	1.4–2 cm diameter
	Blooming season	March to April
	Scent	Strongly ill-scented (reminiscent of cat urine)
Habitat		Mixed-grass wet prairies, wet flatwoods, seepage slopes, stream-side seeps, and wet prairie **ecotones** of dome swamps and depression marshes
Elevation		0–300 m

SOURCE: EFLORAS.ORG

Productive nectar glands advertising an intoxicating drink to flying insects.

Sarracenia flava.

SARRACENIA LEUCOPHYLLA

Found from Leon and Franklin counties west through much of the panhandle, *Sarracenia leucophylla* is another gorgeous tall native species. Like *Sarracenia flava*, it produces two crops of pitchers. The first set in the spring is usually mediocre. Noncarnivorous phyllodia follow, with the second set of carnivorous pitchers not being made until the late summer or early fall. These are the impressively large and robust plants pictured in sellers' ads.

The top third of the plant is full of white areolae, like stained glass from a cathedral. Florists are most likely to use these pitchers in floral arrangements. The problem, of course, is that pitcher plants use their pitchers to obtain necessary nutrients. When the pitches are cut off (all of them or just a few), it stunts the growth of the plant. It is not a sustainable behavior, and it would be best if you didn't support businesses that participate in the trade of cut pitchers. It would be even better if you educated those florists who do participate in this heinous act. In addition to that setback, *Sarracenia leucophylla* habitats are being destroyed due to land development to meet the needs of a growing population. Fire suppression is also causing noncarnivorous plants to outgrow and outcompete *Sarracenia* species.

The lip is like *Sarracenia flava*, while the lid is frilly and has many hairs on the underside that aid in the trapping of insects. The plant has pink to dark red flowers and gets its name from the Greek epithet meaning "white leaf."

Sarracenia leucophylla

Scientific name		*Sarracenia leucophylla*
Synonyms		Swamp lily, white top pitcher plant, white trumpet, crimson pitcher plant
Florida status		Endangered
Florida distribution		Bay, Calhoun, Escambia, Franklin, Gulf, Holmes, Liberty, Okaloosa, Santa Rosa, Walton
United States range		*Sarracenia leucophylla* is only found along the Gulf Coastal Plain, from the Florida Panhandle west to southeastern Mississippi, extending north into extreme southwestern Georgia
Plant characteristics		Forms dense clumps
Pitcher	Color	Green at the base and fades into white with red and green venation
	Height	40–70 cm
	Stature	Erect and tubular
	Areolae	Present
	Rim color	White to green or reddish, flaring and loosely revolute
Phyllodia		5–6, erect
Scapes		30–80 cm
Flower	Color	Bright crimson or maroon
	Seed capsules	1.5–2 cm diameter
	Blooming season	March to May
	Scent	Slightly fragrant
Habitat		Mixed-grass wet prairies, wet flatwoods, seepage slopes, streamside seeps, wet prairie ecotones of dome swamps and depression marshes
Elevation		0–90 m

SOURCE: EFLORAS.ORG

Sarracenia leucophylla.

Sarracenia leucophylla with green anole visiting. JOHN BRUEGGEN

SARRACENIA MINOR

This plant, and its offspring, always put a smile on my face. I once read it described as the ultimate horticultural hoodie. I don't know what that means, but its common name is the hooded pitcher plant due to a cloaked, villainous, shifty appearance. I do see the devious hood, and underneath is a sinister wide-mouthed smile.

One of *Sarracenia minor* most popular descendants is the cultivar named 'Bug Bat'. This is a tall, complex cross with copper-colored pitchers that have rounded arching reddish hoods—a definite clue that it contains *Sarracenia minor* in its pedigree. 'Bug Bat' forms dense colonies, and when I bring my specimen plant to shows, I can easily sell the inexpensive tissue cultured yearlings. People love this look and the fact that they are so cheap (five to ten dollars for a plant in a three-inch pot).

The pure species of *Sarracenia minor* has many white spots on the upper portion of the traps. The hood is smooth. Insects on the underside of the hood or inside the pitcher confuse the sunlight shining in for exits and get disoriented. The slippery windows cause the prey to fall into the vat of digestive enzymes. *Sarracenia minor* produces only carnivorous leaves (no phyllodia) that are quite short, giving it the Latin epithet *minor*.

Sarracenia minor in St. Johns County. JOHN BRUEGGEN

Sarracenia minor is Florida's most widespread and southernmost-occurring species of *Sarracenia*. It can be found as far south as St. Lucie and Okeechobee County, though in extremely few numbers. Its southern population may be extinct now due to development. In Wakulla County, where *Sarracenia minor* and *Sarracenia pstitticina* ranges overlap, hybrids known as ×*formosa* occur. This cross is unique since *Sarracenia minor* are not usually found in overly saturated soils. *Sarracenia psittacina*, on the other hand, can be found floating in streams, fully submerged. Plants of *S.* ×*formosa* that are found in very wet areas must have used their *S. psittacina* genes to survive, which is a cool case of **heterosis** or hybrid vigor.

Sarracenia minor

Scientific name		*Sarracenia minor*
Synonyms		Hooded pitcher plant
Florida status		Threatened
Florida distribution		Alachua, Baker, Brevard, Clay, Columbia, Dixie, Duval, Flagler, Franklin, Gadsden, Gilchrist, Gulf, Hamilton, Hardee, Highlands, Hillsborough, Indian River, Jefferson, Lafayette, Lake, Leon, Levy, Liberty, Madison, Marion, Nassau, Okeechobee, Orange, Osceola, Pasco, Polk, Putnam, St. Johns, St. Lucie, Sumter, Taylor, Union, Volusia, Wakulla
United States range		*Sarracenia minor* can be found in the Atlantic and Gulf Coastal Plains from southern North Carolina into northern Florida
Plant characteristics		Forms dense clumps
Pitcher	Color	Green or suffused with red
	Height	15–25 cm
	Stature	Erect
	Areolae	Prominent, circular
	Rim color	Red, strongly revolute
Phyllodia		No
Scapes		12–55 cm, shorter than longest pitchers
Flower	Color	Yellowish-green
	Seed capsules	0.8–1.8 cm diameter
	Blooming season	April to May
	Scent	Odorless or faintly fragrant
Habitat		Mesic flatwoods, seepage slopes, cutthroat grass wet prairies, margins of depression marshes and dome swamps, seepage ecotone between dry prairies and wet prairies
Elevation		0–90 m

SOURCE: EFLORAS.ORG

Sarracenia minor.

Sarracenia minor in St. Johns County.
JOHN BRUEGGEN

SARRACENIA PSITTACINA

While most carnivorous plants in this book enjoy being kept in wet conditions, *Sarracenia psittacina* can really thrive in them. Occurring in habitats that experience flooding periodically, *Sarracenia psittacina* helps make the case that these plants are carnivorous rather than insectivorous. Due to its semiaquatic habit range and unique lobster pot trap, *Sarracenia psittacina* expands the prey menu from bugs to small fish and crustaceans and even tadpoles.

The **decumbent** rosette of pitchers that rest on the surface of the ground makes it easy to identify this species. The leaves are reddish-green with white areolae. A tiny hole, which some say resembles a parrot's beak, is the only entrance to the trap. The opening's thick secretions of nectar attract terrestrial and aquatic prey, like ants and water fleas. Once inside, the animals are confused by the windows, and the hairs guide them farther into the digestive enzymes at the end of the maze.

While the range of *Sarracenia psittacina* includes wet fields with pines and cypress to truly submerged environments, the extra-large variants are found in flooded areas like Apalachicola National Forest, Okefenokee Swamp, and the Eglin Air Force Base in the Florida Panhandle. If you are going to purchase a variety of *Sarracenia psittacina*, invest a few extra dollars for var. *okefenokeensis*, whose characteristic thirty-centimeter-plus pitchers are impressive to all.

Sarracenia psittacina

Scientific name		*Sarracenia psittacina*
Synonyms		Parrot pitcher
Florida status		Threatened
Florida distribution		Baker, Bay, Calhoun, Escambia, Franklin, Gadsden, Gulf, Holmes, Jackson, Leon, Liberty, Nassau, Okaloosa, Santa Rosa, Wakulla, Walton, Washington
United States range		*Sarracenia psittacina* can be found from southeastern Louisiana east to the Florida Panhandle and north into southern Georgia
Plant characteristics		Forms dense clumps or mats
Pitcher	Color	Reddish-green with white speckles
	Height	8–30 cm
	Stature	Decumbent to semierect
	Areolae	Present
	Rim color	Green, turned inward like a parrot beak, forming one-way lobster trap entrance
Phyllodia		Absent
Scapes		15–35 cm, mostly longer than pitchers
Flower	Color	Sepals maroon, 1.5–2.5 cm × 1–2 cm; petals maroon-red
	Seed capsules	1 cm diameter
	Blooming season	April to May
	Scent	Slightly fragrant
Habitat		Margins of depression marshes and dome swamps, low areas in mesic flatwoods, wet flatwoods, mixed-grass and open-water wet prairies, seepage stream bogs, streamside seep, edge of basin swamps
Elevation		0–60 m

SOURCE: EFLORAS.ORG

An inexpensive and readily available hybrid including *Sarracenia psittacina* is ×*wrigleyana*. This is a naturally occurring hybrid with *Sarracenia leucophylla*, which has been selected for and mass-produced through tissue culture. Pitchers can last for two years and do well in a variety of environments, including sun to part shade and wet to dry conditions. Due to their short, compact stature, they make a great addition to the front of a bog garden.

Due to its decumbent nature, *Sarracenia psittacina*'s dark red to purple-colored flowers are often the only visible portion of the plant when scouting for them in the wilds of Florida.

Sarracenia psittacina.

Sarracenia psittacina.

SARRACENIA ROSEA

Very similar to *Sarracenia purpurea*, *Sarracenia rosea* has thicker lips (2.6–7.5 mm compared to 0.7–3.1 mm). And if you don't want to get the ruler out, *Sarracenia rosea* is the only *Sarracenia* species with pink petals. (Some hybrids of *Sarracenia* can also have pink petals.) The petals of *Sarracenia purpurea* are brick-red to purplish-red and smaller. *Sarracenia rosea* flowers are also on shorter **peduncles** (16–35 cm) compared to *Sarracenia purpurea* (22–79 cm). In addition to flower differences, scientists have separated them into distinct species as their ranges do not overlap.

Sarracenia rosea can be found in counties bordering the east side of the Apalachicola River and west through the panhandle. The pitchers of *Sarracenia rosea* are decumbent but much chubbier than *Sarracenia pstitticina*, making it another easy species to identify.

Both *Sarracenia purpurea* and *Sarracenia rosea* are attractive and simple to grow. Unlike the other species, these can easily be grown indoors with grow lights. The taller species would need their grow lights adjusted frequently. Once you set the grow light for these short pitchers, you are good to go. Another difference is that these pitcher plants don't have a lid that prevents rainwater from filling

Sarracenia 'Fat Chance'.

the pitcher and tipping the plant over. Instead, these decumbent pitchers are so low to the ground that having a lid was not selected for. They have evolved to have a nectar collar, which funnels the rainwater into the pitchers. If you have a dry summer, these low-laying pitchers will appreciate overhead watering, which is unnecessary for the other *Sarracenia* in this chapter and the other carnivorous plants in this book.

Sarracenia 'Fat Chance' is a *Sarracenia rosea* cultivar known for its short, plump, red pitchers. Hobbyists love this one, as it is quite different from other species and hybrids and makes a great addition to the front of any bog. This tissue culture is so popular I've seen nurseries that don't specialize in carnivorous plants carry them.

Sarracenia ×*catesbaei*, another popular tissue culture, is a cross between *Sarracenia flava* and *Sarracenia purpurea*. Since *Sarracenia rosea* separated from *Sarracenia purpurea* into its own species, the cross between *Sarracenia flava* and *Sarracenia rosea* is now referred to as *Sarracenia* ×*naczii*. This hybrid was named in honor of botanist Dr. Robert F. C. Naczi, who recognized the characteristics that led to the separation of *Sarracenia rosea* as a distinct species. *S.* ×*naczii* is more robust and stockier than *S.* ×*catesbaei*. Due to the *Sarracenia rosea* parentage, the rim will most likely be thicker. Due to *Sarracenia flava's* variation, a lot of expressions are common in this hybrid.

A beautiful specimen of *Sarracenia* ×*catesbaei* that I saw at Kew Royal Botanical Gardens.

Sarracenia rosea.
VICTOR A. ALBERT

51

Like many *Sarracenia*, the more sun these plants are exposed to, the more vibrant the pitchers become. Plants grown in shade are mostly green. The Latin epithet *rosea* refers to the pink (rose) flowers, not the red pitchers.

Sarracenia rosea

Scientific name		*Sarracenia rosea*
Basionym/synonyms		*Sarracenia purpurea* var. *burkii*, decumbent pitcher plant, gulf purple pitcher plant, purple pitcher plant
Florida status		Threatened
Florida distribution		Bay, Calhoun, Escambia, Franklin, Gadsden, Holmes, Liberty, Okaloosa, Santa Rosa, Walton, Washington
United States range		Coastal plain in southwestern Georgia, the Florida Panhandle, southern Alabama, southeastern Mississippi
Plant characteristics		Forms dense clumps
Pitcher	Color	Pale green suffused with dull purple-red, frequently with darker reticulated red veins
	Height	6–28 cm
	Stature	Decumbent to ascending
	Areolae	Absent
	Rim color	Red to maroon, thick, flaring
Phyllodia		Absent
Scapes		16–35 cm, longer than pitchers
Flower	Color	Sepals deep purple-red, 3–4.7 cm × 1.7–3.8 cm; petals pale to deep pink to nearly white
	Seed capsules	1.5–2 cm diameter
	Blooming season	March to April
	Scent	Moderately mixed fragrant and ill-scented
Habitat		Streamside seeps, seepage slopes, seepage stream bogs, wet prairies, wet flatwoods
Elevation		0–100 m

SOURCE: EFLORAS.ORG

Sarracenia rosea.

Sarracenia ×naczii. Before *Sarracenia rosea* was described as separate from *Sarracenia purpurea*, this would have been known as *Sarracenia ×catesbaei.*

BILL MCLAUGHLIN

SARRACENIA RUBRA SUBSP. *GULFENSIS*

Unlike the other sections in this chapter, you will notice that simple *Sarracenia rubra* is not listed—only its subspecies. That is because *Sarracenia rubra* now has an autonym, which is *Sarracenia rubra* subsp. *rubra*, and that is not found in Florida.

Truly robust stands of *Sarracenia rubra* subsp. *gulfensis* are only found in sunny areas, open and free from taller foliage. Individuals found in shaded areas have weak, **etiolated** pitchers. There is a large gap between the pointed, rolling, coppery lids and the mouth. The thin lip drops into a spouted "v" like a pitcher of tea. A narrow wing, reminiscent of a zipper, runs the length of the pitcher. They are sometimes found on floating sphagnum mats in swamps. The more sun they are provided, the more contrast can be seen in their maroon veining. Small, dark-colored plants occur in sandy sites. When adding *Sarracenia rubra* subsp. *gulfensis* to a display, consider that they are often the last pitcher plants to go dormant. They look good throughout the fall. In early spring they produce rosy red flowers that have a light rosy scent. The Latin epithet rubra means "red."

Anthocyanin-free plants are sometimes available for cultivation under the name *Sarracenia rubra* subsp. *gulfensis* f. *luteoviridis* or *Sarracenia rubra* subsp. *gulfensis* 'AC Free'. All-green plants have been found in Santa Rosa County.

Sarracenia rubra subsp. *gulfensis*.

Sarracenia rubra subsp. *gulfensis*.

Sarracenia rubra subsp. *gulfensis*

Scientific name		*Sarracenia rubra* subsp. *gulfensis*
Synonyms		Sweet pitcher plant, red pitcher plant, Gulf Coast red pitcher plant, Schnell's pitcher plant
Florida status		Threatened
Florida distribution		Escambia, Okaloosa, Santa Rosa, Walton
United States range		West of the Choctawhatchee River, Florida, and north just into Alabama
Plant characteristics		Forms dense clumps
Pitcher	Color	Green or orange-red in color with red venation
	Height	25–52 cm
	Stature	Erect and tubular
	Areolae	Absent
Phyllodia		Absent
Scapes		26–75 cm
Flower	Color	Crimson to maroon
	Blooming season	April
	Scent	Rosy
Habitat		Wet pine flatwoods, sandy flats, pine and seepage slopes, streams, boggy stream heads, sphagnum swamps
Elevation		60–100 m

SOURCE: EFLORAS.ORG

Florida's Sarracenia Dichotomous Key

1	Pitchers with white areolae on hoods or tubes	>2
1	Pitchers without white areolae on hoods and tubes	>4
2	Pitchers sprawling, decumbent, or, sometimes ascending; mouths located underneath parrot-beak hoods; petals maroon-red	*Sarracenia psittacina*
2	Pitchers erect; petals maroon to red or yellow	>3
3	Pitchers with areas of white areolae around tube and throughout hood; hoods curved backwards **adaxially**, held well beyond mouth; petals maroon to red.	*Sarracenia leucophylla*
3	Pitchers with prominent circular white areolae located on the opposite side of mouth; hood curved, arching closely over mouth; petals yellow.	*Sarracenia minor*
4	Decumbent short squat pitchers, petals pale to deep pink to nearly white	*Sarracenia rosea*
4	Tall erect pitchers, hoods curved backwards adaxially, covering mouth	>5
5	Hood lobes strongly reflexed in that the opposite margins touch or nearly touch; seasonal erect phyllodia	*Sarracenia flava*
5	Red veining on surface of pitchers; phyllodia absent year-round	>6
6	Gradually tapering pitchers from base to mouth with slight distal bulge. Found west of the Choctawhatchee River	*Sarracenia rubra* subsp. *gulfensis*
6	Monomorphic dull green pitchers in spring and summer. Found east of the Perdido River in northwestern Escambia County	*Sarracenia alabamensis* subsp. *wherryi*

Commonly cared-for carnivores. Look for these to add to your collection.

Sarracenia leucophylla. JOHN BRUEGGEN

Sarracenia 'Reptilian Rose'. MAGGIE CHEN

Sarracenia rosea. BILL MCLAUGHLIN

Sarracenia ×Mardi Gras.

Sarracenia 'Adrian Slack'. MAGGIE CHEN

Sarracenia 'Fat Chance'.

Bladderworts

Utricularia are **floriferous**. It is remarkable to see en masse flowering of *Utricularia cornuta* or *Utricularia purpurea* in the Floridian wilderness. The carpet of yellow or purple flowers appears to be unending. However, having one or two plugs of each species in your personal collection will probably not impress the neighbors. For some it's more of a "got to catch 'em all" attitude. For others it is an enjoyable botanical challenge. Most Florida *Utricularia* species are cosmopolitans and do well in the same growing conditions as your other carnivorous plants with little additional effort. For much of the year, many of the terrestrial *Utricularia* will look like nothing more than tiny blades of grass. The aquatic species will resemble floating blobs of algae. To the trained eye, they are intricate, and deadly, predators. To the historian, they are imbued with scientific conflict and subsequent progress.

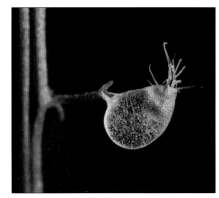

Utricularia gibba. BOAZ NG

Known as the fastest, yet smallest, carnivorous plant in the world, *Utricularia* predation tactics are astonishing. The Latin epithet for *Utricularia* means "small bag." But these small-bag traps are the most sophisticated of all carnivorous plants. With bladders ranging in size from one to six millimeters long, these elastic walls can vacuum up prey in less than one millisecond. On the outside of the trapdoor are long hairs that guide the prey to the door and shorter trigger hairs that line the door. The traps are filled with liquid. Glands pump out fluid, which creates a negative pressure system. When the trap door is triggered, it flies inward and vacuums up the prey and surrounding liquid, and the trapdoor is reset. Digestive enzymes are then pumped into the bladder. Depending on the size of the bladder and the size of the prey, digestion can take a few hours to a few days. When extra-large prey are caught partially inside the trap, they are digested bit by bit. This is excellently animated in my TED-Ed video titled "The Wild World of Carnivorous Plants."

While there are epiphytic *Utricularia* species around the world, in Florida we only have aquatic and terrestrial species. Aquatic *Utricularia* species are usually found in nutrient-poor water systems. They can be found in shallow standing bodies of water or in deeper ponds, streams, or ditches. Some aquatic species like to anchor down, while others float carelessly. In favorable conditions, some species can grow three or four apical leaf nodes per day, while their shoot bases decay at the same expeditious rate. One leaf can have dozens to hundreds of two-cell-thick predatory bladders. On the inside of the trap are two types of glands. Large glands secrete digestive enzymes, while the smaller upfront glands pump out water. Aquatic prey range in size from 0.5 to 2 millimeters long. Despite their tiny volumetric size, *Utricularia*, like *Sarracenia*, have commensal microorganisms living inside the traps. Algae, bacteria, ciliates, cyanobacteria, dinophytes, euglens, microfungi, and rotifers all move in to the originally sterile traps. Once inside, they participate in the decomposition of the prey items. Some microorganisms even propagate in the traps. However, due to some methodological limitations, scientists are still confused about which organisms are truly commensals and which turn into prey!

During the plant's life span, only a fraction of traps catch macroscopic prey, while all of them contain communities of microbial commensals. This has caused some scientists to question if *Utricularia* are hunters or farmers. Recently it was discovered that the best term for these plants would be *omnivores*. With over one hundred algae species found in the traps of *Utricularia* species, it was found that bladderworts can cultivate, harvest, digest, and utilize the organic plant and animal matter. This finding was published in 2018, but *Utricularia* have interested scientists for hundreds of years.

In 1797, James Sowerby, an English artist and natural historian, believed the bladders served as flotation devices and that insects lodged inside them for protection. Then a few studies that involved cutting off all the bladders revealed that the remaining plant still floated. In 1858, the Crouan brothers, French amateur botanists, also recorded small aquatic animals within the bladders. This made headlines, and Darwin read their paper and became very interested. A few years later, scientists around the world were making similar observations.

Ferdinand Cohn, a German biologist, was impressed by Darwin's work on insectivorous plants and convinced himself that *Utricularia* was another carnivorous species. He corresponded with Darwin about the prospect. They knew that dead microorganisms were found in the bladders but didn't know how they entered. Darwin and his son fixed human hair, grass, and lead shavings to handles and placed them near the *Utricularia*'s opening. "They disappeared so suddenly that, not seeing what had happened, I thought that I had fitted them off," Darwin writes. Darwin knew that *Dionaea*, *Drosera*, and *Pinguicula* captured or digested their prey by active movement. But he couldn't understand how *Utricularia* did it. Since he could not trigger the bladder's opening with a needle or camel-hair brush, he concluded that the animals were forcing themselves in the bladders for protection or in search of food, using their heads like a wedge.

Cohn placed water fleas in an aquarium or petri dish with *Utricularia* and observed the bladders filled with fleas the next morning. He concluded, independently of Darwin, that the fleas were forcing themselves into the bladder.

Earlier, in 1871, Mary Treat sent Charles Darwin a letter at the request of their mutual friend Asa Gray. Gray was a professor of botany at Harvard University and corresponded with Charles Darwin regularly. He had first met him when Joseph Dalton Hooker introduced them at Kew Gardens in 1839.

Utricularia olivacea (left) and *U. gibba* (right). LEIF GUNNAR BOMAN

While Treat's first correspondence was about the sexes of butterflies and the carnivorous *Drosera anglica*, their letters progressed into other carnivorous plants, including *Drosera filiformis*, Venus flytraps, *Sarracenia*, *Pinguicula*, and finally *Utricularia*.

In a letter dated December 2, 1874, Treat wrote to Darwin:

> I have been studying the bladder-bearing species of *Utricularia* off and on the last year, and am now fully satisfied that they are the most wonderful carnivorous plants that I have yet seen. . . .
>
> Last evening I found one just incarcerated in a very transparent bladder, it being the sole occupant. It was very active with its telescopic feet and horns, but in the morning—some twelve hours having elapsed since my last observation—it had no longer the power of thrusting its feet in and out, it could only move the brush-like appendages, and a slow movement was visible in the dark intestine that traverses the length of the body; and now this evening, twenty-four hours having passed, no movement is visible in any part of the animal, but it is slowly disintegrating.
>
> This is the history of many specimens that I have watched in the same way.
>
> I never knew, not even a small animalcule to escape after once inside the bladder.
>
> I have not heard of anyone making observations on these plants, and so I thought mine of sufficient importance to announce to you.

In Darwin's 1875 book *Insectivorous Plants*, he wrongly concluded from his experiments on *Utricularia neglecta* that the valve was not sensitive to irritation. Treat had published her accurate observations in the February 1876 issue of *Harper's New Monthly* magazine. On June 1, 1876, Darwin wrote to Treat: "It certainly appears from your excellent observations that the valve was sensitive . . . but I cannot understand why I could never with all my pains excite any movement. It is pretty clear I am quite wrong about the head acting like a wedge."

For more letters with Darwin, check out the Darwin Correspondence Project from the University of Cambridge. With more than fifteen thousand letters and two thousand correspondents from around the world, it is a humbling reminder that science is a team sport, and collaboration is essential to understanding our world.

Although these scientific colleagues were not 100 percent correct about the trapping mechanisms of *Utricularia*, their insight has been the basis of significant scientific contributions for over a century.

Growing Your Own Infusoria for Aquatic *Utricularia*

Infusoria is a collective term that includes several freshwater microorganisms, which can comprise cyclops, daphnia, paramecia, protists, and rotifers. All these are tasty treats for aquatic *Utricularia*. Infusoria can be cultivated in many ways. Here is one of the easier setups:

- Chop up a variety of vegetables, like cucumber skins, kale, broccoli stems, and peas.
- Pour boiling water over the vegetables or microwave them in water for one minute.
- Let the vegetables cool to room temperature.
- Add vegetables to a glass jar or container.
- Cover the vegetables with water from a fish aquarium or pond to near capacity.
- Leave the jar uncovered or place a lid with holes on the jar.
- Place the jar in a brightly lit window.

This will encourage decomposition and algae growth, which the infusoria feed on. In a few days, you'll notice the water has become cloudy. The vegetables may float and then sink after several days. The liquid may smell, and a layer of scum can form. This is normal. After the bacteria blooms, the infusoria population will grow exponentially. As the water clears, the odor will reduce to a neutral smell. The streaming clouds that remain will be the infusoria. This entire process can take two to six weeks. Create infusoria cultures in succession so you always have a population to feed to your aquatic *Utricularia*. Use a turkey baster or eye dropper to transfer the infusoria to your hungry plants.

UTRICULARIA AMETHYSTINA— FLORIDA PURPLE BLADDERWORT

Historically found in Lee and Collier counties, this species is probably now **extirpated** within Florida due to human encroachment. It was only recorded in the state several decades ago and might have been lost with the development of I-75. It could still be in Florida, as it is highly **polymorphic** and would be difficult to find when not in flower and still tough to identify when in flower. Found in flooded areas, it is a semiaquatic terrestrial. It is also natively found in Bolivia, Brazil, Guyana, and Peru. *Utricularia amethystina* flowers can range in color from white to pale yellow to whitish-purple. This species is not readily available for cultivation, most likely due to lack of interest.

Utricularia amethystina. MAURICIO MERCADANTE

UTRICULARIA CORNUTA—HORNED BLADDERWORT

Reported statewide, this species is easily spotted during and after the summer rainy season. As the water recedes, two to five yellow flowers appear on leafless yellow-green scapes, which can grow up to twelve inches. Plants flower from June to September and interestingly earlier if *Utricularia juncea* is present. *Utricularia juncea* usually has a purple-green scape that is shorter and produces smaller flowers. This is a good bog garden choice if you can find plugs from a native or wildflower nursery. Don't purchase seeds from abroad, as you'll probably be conned into broccoli seeds.

Utricularia cornuta. ALEX ROUKAS

UTRICULARIA FLORIDANA—FLORIDA BLADDERWORT

Utricularia floridana is a large, perennial, aquatic bladderwort that I have had success with growing in large jars and glass containers. Grown in full sun, it does best with other aquatic plants that help buffer the water conditions. Water lilies, frogbit, pickerel weed, water chestnuts, and other *Utricularia* species make good companions. Yellow flowers occur during the summer. The plant forms **turions** when temperatures dip below 45°F. These winter buds help it survive the winter, lying dormant in the leaf litter until the water warms up again. *Utricularia floridana* can also be grown successfully indoors in an aquarium with a grow light. When available, small segments of this species retail for around ten to fifteen dollars.

Utricularia floridana. ALAN CRESSLER

UTRICULARIA FOLIOSA—
LEAFY BLADDERWORT

A large, suspended aquatic found throughout North and South America and Africa, this carnivorous plant flowers throughout the year. Found in a variety of habitats ranging from slowly flowing waters to deep lakes, this species is not easily available for cultivation. If available, it was probably poached.

UTRICULARIA GIBBA—HUMPED
OR FLOATING BLADDERWORT

Found statewide, this worldly cosmopolitan is readily available for the hobbyist. Growing in temperate and tropical climates, *Utricularia gibba* is the beginner's choice for those wishing to grow one aquatic species. It can be grown in a bucket outside, in a glass jar on the windowsill, or under grow lights. If you are growing other carnivorous plants using the tray method, you can grow *Utricularia gibba* in the few inches of water that the other plants sit in. Flowering between June and September, it is recognized by its small yellow flowers held at a forty-five-degree angle. A couple of segments range in price from five to fifteen dollars. You shouldn't need much more than that to start with, as they will multiply easily in Florida.

Utricularia foliosa. LEIF GUNNAR BOMAN

Utricularia gibba. ALAN CRESSLER

Utricularia inflata. ALAN CRESSLER

UTRICULARIA INFLATA—
SWOLLEN BLADDERWORT

Along with *Utricularia radiata*, these unique plants produce a rosette of starlike floatation arms in which their flowers grow. *Utricularia inflata* produces four to ten spokes with arms that taper at both ends—unlike *Utricularia radiata*, which has cylindrical floating arms. *Utricularia inflata* is a perennial and only goes dormant during freezing temperatures. Occurring in acidic ponds and slow-moving streams, this species can be found statewide. They are a spectacular wildflower but not regularly available for the hobbyist.

UTRICULARIA JUNCEA—
SOUTHERN BLADDERWORT

Almost identical to *Utricularia cornuta* but smaller, *Utricularia juncea*'s canary-yellow blooms are about half an inch long and without the hood as seen in *Utricularia cornuta*. The horn is also much shorter (six millimeters compared to over fourteen millimeters). Common to most of Florida, *Utricularia juncea* and other species are hard to locate when not in bloom.

UTRICULARIA OLIVACEA—
PIEDMONT BLADDERWORT

A very small flowering plant, *Utricularia olivacea* is so unassuming I almost couldn't find a worthy picture for this book. Measuring less than 1 millimeter across, and on scapes only 2 to 2.5 centimeters tall, flowers occur from September to late October. It is the only white flowering *Utricularia* in Florida.

Utricularia juncea. E. P. MALLORY

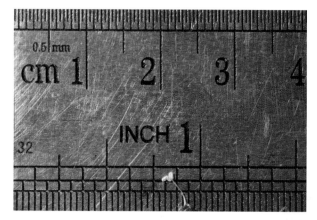

Utricularia olivacea.
LEIF GUNNAR BOMAN

UTRICULARIA PURPUREA—
EASTERN PURPLE BLADDERWORT

Found throughout the state in shallow freshwater habitats, the snapdragon-looking flowers are deep purple with the lower lips pouchlike. *Utricularia purpurea* has no foliage and will only go dormant during freezes. The long brown whorls of bladders float suspended in the water column.

Utricularia purpurea. ALAN CRESSLER

UTRICULARIA RADIATA—
LITTLE FLOATING BLADDERWORT

This species is like *Utricularia inflata* but is smaller and has fewer arms.

Utricularia inflata (left) versus *U. radiata* (right). LEIF GUNNAR BOMAN

UTRICULARIA RESUPINATA—
LAVENDER BLADDERWORT,
SMALL PURPLE
BLADDERWORT

Found statewide, *Utricularia resupinata* is frequently found in wet flatwoods and pond margins. Easily distinguished from the other three purple/lavender flowering Florida species, *Utricularia resupinata* has an upward-curving lower lip. The ruffled flowers have a yellow throat, and the lower lip is not **saccate** like *Utricularia purpurea*. Flowers occur after flooding recedes.

Utricularia resupinata. ALAN CRESSLER

UTRICULARIA SIMULANS—
FRINGED BLADDERWORT

Flowers have **fimbriate** (tooth- or feather-edged) bracts and sepals. Flowers occur throughout the year in moist pinelands.

Utricularia simulans. E. P. MALLORY

UTRICULARIA STRIATA—
STRIPED BLADDERWORT

Found in northern Florida, this affixed subaquatic produces a yellow **corolla** with red streaks at the base of the lower lip.

Utricularia striata. ALAN CRESSLER

UTRICULARIA SUBULATA—
ZIGZAG BLADDERWORT

Ubiquitous in the wild and in cultivation, this tiny wildflower sits on an interesting zigzag scape and is commonly seen throughout the wet flatwoods of Florida. The lower lip of the corolla is far larger than the upper. This is our smallest yellow terrestrial species. In addition to flowering, it can reproduce through the phenomenon known as **cleistogamy**. This is when copious amounts of seedpods are produced without flowers opening. Other plants known to self-pollinate include peanuts, peas, and violas. A plug of *Utricularia subulata* can be purchased for under ten dollars. The plugs can be added to backyard bogs, terrariums, greenhouses, and on windowsills. Caveat emptor: they spread, everywhere. If you have carnivorous plant soil, they will grow in it. This may be fine for the *Sarracenia* hobbyist, but if you are trying to keep *Utricularia* species in pure species pots, you may find yourself overrun with zigzagging flowers.

Utriculata subulata. JIM FOWLER

Commonly cared-for carnivores. Look for these to add to your collection.

Utricularia purpurea. ALEX ROUKIS

Utricularia gibba.

Utricularia floridana.

Utricularia inflata.

Flower Color	Species	Size	Ecosystem	Lifecycle	Habitat	Flower #/ raceme	Flower Season	Trap Length (mm)
Purple	U. amethystina	Small to medium	Terrestrial	Annual or perennial	Wet sandy savanna, peaty swamps, in damp soil among rocks and by streams. Pine flatwoods	1–10	Throughout the year	1–1.2
Purple	U. purpurea	Medium	Suspended aquatic	Perennial	Shallow to deep pools, and slow flowing streams	1–3	February to October	1–2
Purple	U. resupinata	Small	Affixed subaquatic	Perennial	In shallow water, in sand or mud, over much of its range in open pine savanna	1 (rarely 2)	February to September	0.5–1
White	U. olivacea	Minute	Suspended aquatic	Annual	Still or slowly flowing water in ponds, lakes, ditches, streams. Often in association with other submerged aquatics and some-times forming pure floating mats.	2–5	Spring and Autumn	0.3–0.8
Yellow	U. foliosa	Large, robust	Suspended aquatic.	Perennial	Still or slowly flowing, shallow to deep water in lakes, rivers, marshes and ditches	3–20	Throughout the year	1–2
Yellow	U. gibba	Small to medium	Affixed or suspended aquatic.	Annual or perennial	Grows freely on bottom or other vegetation, usually in tangled mats	1–12	Throughout the year	1–2.5
Yellow	U. radiata	Medium	Suspended aquatic	Annual or perennial	Lakes, pools, swamps & ditches in still, deep to shallow water	3–4	February to October	0.7–2
Yellow	U. simulans	Small to medium	Terrestrial	Perennial	Wet, usually sandy soil in open savanna vegetation. Pine flatwoods	2–10	Flowers during the wet season or early dry season.	0.2–0.3
Yellow	U. subulata	Small to very small	Terrestrial	Annual	Wet sandy savanna, damp shal-low soil over rocks, ditches, stream and pool sides and damp places generally in low open vegetation	1–25	Flowers when habitat is wet	0.2–0.7
Yellow	U. cornuta	Small to medium	Terrestrial or subaquatic	Perennial	Marshes, swamps & pools, often in shallow water, mostly at low altitude. Along lake margins, pine flatwoods	1–6	February to June	0.3–0.8
Yellow	U. floridana	Large	Affixed aquatic	Perennial	Usually in water 30 cm to 1 m deep, in lakes containing very little other vegetation. Appears to be floating, but is actually rooted. Can be so abundant that it is the dominant plant of a site.	5–20	July to August	1.5–3
Yellow	U. inflata	Large	Suspended aquatic.	Perennial	Lakes, pools, swamps and ditches in shallow to deep water	9–14	January to June	1–3
Yellow	U. juncea	Small to medium	Terrestrial	Perennial	Wet savanna, marshes, swamps and by pools and streams, often in shallow water	1–12	August to November	0.3–0.6
Yellow	U. striata	Medium	Affixed subaquatic	Perennial	In shallow (a few cm deep) water, and on wet soil, in bogs and by pools, and on floating mats of other aquatic plants (e.g. Sphagnum spp.) in deeper water	1–6	April to September	0.6–1.5

SOURCE: *THE GENUS UTRICULARIA: A TAXONOMIC MONOGRAPH* BY PETER TAYLOR

Corolla Color	Upper Lip	Lower Lip	Corolla Size (cm)	Endemic to the US	Notes
Violet or mauve with a yellow spot at the base of the lower lip but very variable and may be wholly white or yellow. Polymorphic.	Oblong or oblong-**elliptic**	**Transversely obovate**	0.3–2	No	May be extinct in Florida due to development. More tolerant of shade than most terrestrial *Utricularia* species. Leaves in a rosette.
Purple with a yellow blotch at the base of the lower lip	Convex, approximately circular	3-lobed, the lateral lobes saccate, the midlobe longer	0.8–1.8	No	Leaves are in whorls of 4.
Rose pink with a darker spur and a cream spot at the base of the lower lip	Narrowly oblong-obovate	Broadly cuneate with a prominent, **rugulose** swelling in the center	0.6–1	No	Grass-like leaves. Flowers in shallow water, but can be found in deeper water. Flower has a "c" or "e" shape when viewed from the side
Cream white	Convex	Concave, broadly obovate	2–3.5 mm	No	Thin strands with single short leaves. Can be confused with *U. gibba* when not in flower.
Yellow, with sometimes purple nerves	Circular or transversely elliptic	Larger, transversely elliptic to **subreniform**	0.8–1.5	No	Main stem is thick and flat, and then fernlike leaves. Has two distinct leaves: bladder branches and foliar branches.
Yellow, often with reddish-brown nerves	Broadly **ovate** to almost circular, usually ± obscurely to distinctly 3-lobed	Slightly smaller, circular to transversely elliptic	4–25 mm	No	Very small strands with single short leaves. Can be confused with *U. olivacea* when not in flower.
Yellow with brown marks at the base of the lower lip, and brown nerves on the spur	Almost circular	Transversely oblong	0.9–2	Yes	Like *U. inflata*, but smaller. Leaflike branches equal.
Yellow	Broadly ovate	Circular or broadly **trullate**	4–10	No	Needs a substrate which is acidic and with extremely low mineral and organic content. Paddle-like leaves.
2 cm(cleistogamous) or 0.5–1 cm long, yellow or (cleistogamous) white or reddish;	Broadly ovate	Rhombic to broadly cuneate in outline	0.5–2	No	Paddle-like leaves
Yellow	Ovate-oblong to broadly obovate from a narrow oblong base	**Galeate**, approximately circular in outline	1.5–2	No	Similar to *U. juncea*, but larger. Open flowers will overtop unopened flowers that are above
Yellow with red streaks at the base of the lower lip	Almost circular	Smaller, almost circular	2	Yes	Similar to *U. striata*. Foxtail or feather boa-like. Has two distinct leaves: bladder branches and foliar branches.
Yellow with brown marks at the base of the lower lip and brown nerves on the spur	Almost circular	Transversely oblong	2–2.5	Yes	Like *U. radiata*, but larger. Leaflike branches unequal
Yellow	Broadly obovate to approximately circular	Galeate, approximately circular in outline	0.25–1.5	No	Similar to *U. cornuta*. Open flowers will not overtop unopened flowers
Yellow with red streaks at the base of the lower lip	Subreniform	Slightly smaller, almost circular	2	Yes	Similar to *U. floridana*

Butterworts

Pinguicula, or *pings* for those in the know, are generally one of the last genera of carnivorous plants hobbyists add to their collection. This is most likely due to their inactive traps and simple rosette shape. It's a shame too because they are beautiful and at least as interesting as the others. The prey become stuck on the glue-like leaves, drown in the digestive enzymes, and then get absorbed! Doesn't seem like a good way to go if you are a fungus gnat. Now, with a surge in aroid and other houseplants, noncarnivorous growers are seeking these carnivorous companions to help take care of their fruit fly, fungus gnat, and no-see-um problems.

In Latin *pinguicula* means "little greasy one" or "little fat one" due to their buttery or greasy feel. The leaves are covered in minute glandular hairs that each produce a drop of gummy glue. *P. planifolia* looks like a pile of wet sticky tongues when glue production is in full swing. Upon close inspection you will notice a pebbled surface that is studded with tiny **sessile** glands. Root systems are fibrous and fragile, only descending six centimeters. This allows you to grow them on permanently wet, porous rock structures.

In our temperate to subtropical climate in Florida, we have six species of *Pinguicula* that have carnivorous leaves year-round. Many popular Mexican butterworts kept by hobbyist go through a succulent period, where their leaves are incapable of catching insects. Our Florida species are always willing and able to catch small insects. While their leaf size may be reduced in the winter, their overall health and size is most influenced by the availability of water. Most of them look the worst in the hot summer months and best in January to February right before they are about to bloom.

When the plants are not in flower, it is difficult to identify them by their vegetative parts. *P. planifolia* can have red leaves when grown in bright light, but the others look very similar to one another. Many people enjoy growing butterworts in general due to their flowers, regardless of their carnivorous nature. They require pollination to produce seed. If you keep your *Pinguicula* indoors, you may use a paintbrush to pollinate the plant if flying pollinators are not present. Seeds require damp soil and temperatures above 60°F. Germination takes two to four weeks. While they can be kept in brightly lit terrariums, they do best with strong air circulation, which prevents fungus. If cyanobacteria or moss becomes an issue, replant the *Pinguicula* into new growing media.

Pinguicula planifolia. Once you hear it described as wet tongues, it's hard to see anything else. MANNY HERRERA

While many carnivorous plants have popular common names, many of the *Pinguicula* species are known only by their scientific name. This may be a testament to how little the general public knows about them. Since the 2010s, the Brenda Molano-Flores's lab, at the Illinois Natural History Survey, has been publishing new research on the biology and ecology of ping species in Florida. This work has produced much-needed information about the reproductive biology, pollinators, prey capture, anthocyanin's role and production, and population genetics for three *Pinguicula* species: *P. ionantha*, *P. lutea*, and *P. planifolia*.

The Molano-Flores lab has learned that these three species of butterworts need pollinators for the formation of fruits and seeds, in particular bees. They were also able to determine that, depending on the species, the longevity of flowers can be between two to three weeks if they are not pollinated.

In addition, scientists at the lab have learned that the Florida *Pinguicula* species have floral **nastic** movements. The flowers open and close on a daily cycle. Unlike other *Pinguicula* species whose corolla will become immobile and remains open once mature, all six of our native species and a Mexican species close at night and open during the day until the flower fades and sheds. The question, of course, is why.

One reason other plants do this nocturnal "sleeping behavior" is to protect the flower's interior from getting wet. Some of these even close when it is an overcast day or when a cloud hangs over them. But Austrian botanist Andreas Fleischmann does not believe that is true since many other *Pinguicula* species that have similar flower shapes remain open despite heavy rain events.

In addition to closing their flowers at night, the *Pinguicula* species also share a hairy protrusion near the corolla entrance, called a **palate**. These serve as lures to attract specific pollinators, although these structures themselves do not contain any pollen. When the pollinators try to feed on the false pollen, they touch the stigma and anthers that are inside the corolla and pollinate the plant. All is not lost for the pollinator, though, since butterworts do have nectar at the tip of their spur to reward them.

Our native species of *Pinguicula* require pollinators as they are not able to self-pollinate due to their complex flower arrangement. With their thick stems, capable of supporting heavy pollinators, it has been assumed that long-tongued or medium to large bees pollinate our *Pinguicula*. While some species of plants that produce low levels of pollen yield a variety of colors and scents within a species to prevent pollinators from learning which flower species to avoid, "the extent this is also true for the 'pollen-mimicking' but nectar-rewarding *Pinguicula* species is not clear," Fleischmann writes.

Some annual species of *Pinguicula* (*P. lusitanica*, *P. takakii*, and *P. sharpiican*, for example) self-pollinate and set seed.

Pinguicula planifolia growing submerged. SARA JOHNSON

Fleischmann says these species are also uniform in shape and color. They have no need to deceive pollinators, since they do not rely on them to reproduce.

Since little is known about the pollinators of the southeast *Pinguicula* species, we can hypothesize that the plants may be protecting themselves from harmful nightly visitors. But why do other pings not show this behavior? Fleischmann suggests that maybe the nighttime closure serves to prevent pollinators that are active in the early morning and could learn about false pollen displays too quickly. If they visit other plants that have real pollen, they will not become frustrated too quickly. They would still visit the Florida *Pinguicula* later in the day. Fleischmann suggests more field studies to learn about the fascinating flower biology of carnivorous plants in general.

Back in the United States, the Molano-Flores lab has learned that the capture of prey such as springtails (*Collembola* sp.) and very small flies can be affected by habitat management in at least *P. lutea*. Encroachment of habitat has resulted in less prey being captured. They have also found that prey capture in *P. planifolia* is not improved by the red color of its leaves (anthocyanin) compared to green leaves and that environmental factors such as light intensity and soil/water nutrient content will influence foliar anthocyanin production (red color) in this species.

The lab has also learned that *P. ionantha* populations have low levels of genetic diversity, which could affect their fitness and evolutionary capability in the future due to environmental changes. Overall, not only does their research help us to understand aspects of the biology and ecology of this fascinating group of butterworts, but it also provides much-needed information for the conservation of these species in the United States.

PINGUICULA CAERULEA—BLUEFLOWER BUTTERWORT, VIOLET BUTTERWORT

This state-threatened species is one of the easiest to grow of the warm-temperate *Pinguicula* species. It makes an excellent addition to a bog garden. It flowers between January and May and is native to sandy bogs and low pinelands throughout Florida. The flowers have veined petals that are blue to purple with a darker throat. The leaves average a little more than three inches. Pings do well in indirect or filtered light. *Caerulus* in Latin means "from the sky or sea." It can be a bit difficult to find these for sale. When searching the Internet, make sure you type *Pinguicula*, for if you type *P. caerulea* you will most likely get *Passiflora caerulea*, which is an aggressive passionflower vine that is not carnivorous.

Pinguicula caerulea.

Pinguicula caerulea. ALAN CRESSLER

PINGUICULA IONANTHA— GODFREY'S BUTTERWORT

P. ionantha is a rare, endangered butterwort species endemic to the Florida Panhandle. Apalachicola National Forest is home to more than half of the known population. It is found in seepage slopes, bogs, and ecotones between flatwoods and cypress stringers. Roadside ditches and wet prairies are also suitable habitats for this species. It can often be found growing in shallow standing water. What is also remarkable is that it wasn't described as a species until 1961 by Florida State University botanist Robert Kenneth Godfrey.

Pinguicula ionantha.

Pinguicula ionantha. JEAN MENGELKOCH

71

The flowers are lavender to white and best spotted in the field between late February and April. The rosette can grow up to six inches wide. Not too often available for the hobbyist, these plants are short-lived perennials, and many die after a couple of years. It is best to propagate through seed to keep your collection population up.

In the wild this species like the others is experiencing habitat loss due to logging, drainage alteration, and lack of fire.

PINGUICULA LUTEA—YELLOW BUTTERWORT

The only yellow-flowered butterwort found in Florida, *P. lutea* is listed as threatened. When not in bloom, it looks identical to *P. caerulea*. The common name refers to the flower color and the sticky glue on the leaves that traps insects. The leaf edges roll inward, and the tips of the leaves are pointed. It grows in sandy bogs and savannas typically drier than the other species prefer. Rosettes can grow up to six inches wide.

Pinguicula lutea.

Pinguicula lutea in typical flower form. SARA JOHNSON

Pinguicula lutea's flowers are usually straw-yellow to bright yellow, but in rare instances they can be white. SARA JOHNSON

PINGUICULA PLANIFOLIA—
YELLOW-FLOWERED BUTTERWORT, CHAPMAN'S BUTTERWORT

Who doesn't want to see a plant that looks like a pile of tongues? We must save this threatened species! *P. planifolia*, in addition to looking cool, is known for spending much of the year submerged. Flowers emerge from the water between January and March. Blooms can vary from white to pink, lavender, or dark purple. Of the six native species, *P. planifolia* is the only one that when exposed to bright light will increase anthocyanin production and produce red leaves. While the Molano-Flores lab found that red leaves attracted less prey (like springtails) than green leaves, the butterwort may rely on other cues like olfactory cues to attract its prey.

Pinguicula planifolia.

Pinguicula planifolia in typical flower form. SARA JOHNSON

73

PINGUICULA PRIMULIFLORA— SWAMP BUTTERWORT, SOUTHERN BUTTERWORT

This species is the most popular in cultivation of the Florida species. Plants can be found for around ten dollars, and they produce pups at the end of their leaves, so you can propagate them for yourself quite easily. Found in shaded areas of very wet peat and sphagnum, *P. primuliflora* can be grown in wide, shallow containers in filtered light. I've had the best experience in growing them in six-inch pots or vertically half-cut rain barrels and separating the plantlets frequently. They are short-lived and prone to rot, so it is a good idea to keep separate pots as backups.

In the wild most sites have been destroyed, causing this species to be listed as endangered. A few plants remain on the Eglin Air Force Base. They can be seen growing along streams or on islands of mud in rivers. They produce beautiful large colonies as shown in the picture. This is one of my favorite pictures in the entire book.

Pinguicula primuliflora.

Pinguicula primuliflora flourishing on a mud island. ALAN CRESSLER

74

PINGUICULA PUMILA—SMALL BUTTERWORT, BOG VIOLET, DWARF BUTTERWORT

Found in inundated acidic soils with poor nutrients like flatwoods throughout most of Florida, *P. pumila* is the smallest of the Florida butterworts. The rosette of small succulent leaves usually does not exceed three-quarters of an inch! Flowers can be white, blue, violet, or pink. This species is the only one in Florida that does not have a palate that extends beyond the throat of the corolla. The flower is also usually less than three-quarters of an inch including the spur. Flowering occurs throughout the year in frost-free areas.

Pinguicula pumila.

Pinguicula pumila in St. Vincent Island National Wildlife Refuge in Franklin County, Florida, showcasing different flower colors. ALAN CRESSLER

Commonly cared-for carnivores. Look for these to add to your collection.

Pinguicula caerulea.

Pinguicula lutea.

Pinguicula planifolia. ALAN CRESSLER

Pinguicula primuliflora.

Sundews

When customers approach the table full of carnivorous plants for sale, they are quick to dismiss the sundews. They wrongly think the sundews are too delicate to care for. They are afraid they will hurt the fragile plant. Sundews, although jewel-like, are hardy plants, with some Florida species acting like weeds wherever carnivorous plant soil is found.

Sundews use sticky mucilage produced from glands on the tips of **trichomes** found on their leaves to trap their victims—and they are victims. Sundews' numerous stalked glands produce glue that does not dry out when exposed to air, unlike synthetic glues, which has interested researchers. The prey becomes entangled with the leaf, which produces a sticky secretion, causing prey to suffocate. This glue is one of the strongest found in nature and is a water-based polysaccharide. Only after the insect is caught, the plant secretes digestive enzymes into the glue to aid in digestion. Since researchers can't milk sundews (can you imagine?) to reap the benefits of their adhesive, they have invested quite a bit of effort into mimicking their glue production, a process known as biomimicry. Using this bioinspired approach, one group of researchers created a sundew-inspired hydrogel that was confirmed to have superior wound-healing capabilities; they used it to have a "suturing" effect on wound sites.

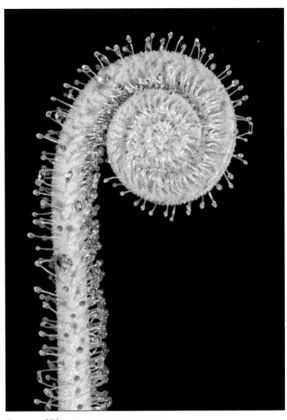

Drosera filiformis. FLORENT CHOUFFOT

Drosera carnivory is easy to see unfold when you see the plants in person. Customers are quick to pick up a three-inch pot and examine the plants' sticky traps, most likely active. The plants are usually scattered with carcasses or struggling insects. Customers are delighted by this and imagine all the bugs they are going to suck up in their kitchen fruit fly–breeding headquarters.

There are more than two hundred species around the world, with five being native to Florida. In Florida they can be found frequently with other carnivorous plants. The ones around the world can range from pygmy penny size to bushes. In Florida, our sundews' leaves range from less than an inch to twenty inches in length.

Spectacular species are still being discovered around the world. Back in 2012, Reginaldo Vasconcelos, an orchid grower, posted a photo of a sundew on Facebook while hiking a mountaintop near his home in southeastern Brazil. A year later scientist Paulo Gonella, a researcher from the University of São Paulo, saw the shared post and recognized it as something special. He and Vasconcelos returned to the  mountain and confirmed it as a new species that is microendemic to the top of that single mountain. Although locally abundant there, it has been classified as critically endangered due to its fragile and isolated habitat. Coffee and eucalyptus plantations in addition to cattle ranching and invasive species of grass are encroaching on this newly discovered species. It's surprising it took so long to discover this species as the newly named *Drosera magnifica* is the largest New World sundew, reaching a height of almost five feet!

In Greek *droseros* means "glistening or dewy."

DROSERA BREVIFOLIA—
DWARF SUNDEW

Drosera brevifolia, the dwarf sundew, has a large range that spans from Uruguay to Virginia. It prefers full sun and wet savannahs with sandy to peaty soil. Averaging the size of a dime to a quarter, its epithet, meaning "short leaf," is easy to understand. There is debate about whether this species is an annual or perennial; *Drosera brevifolia* has adapted its survival strategy based on climatic conditions. In drier conditions it acts as an annual, dying back during the drier summer and setting seed. In Kentucky it may be referred to as a biennial. In late summer to fall in Florida, the plant may resprout from its roots after surviving a dry spring or summer. This plant can be kept alive for many years in cultivation if you cut off the flower stalks as they appear. If you allow it to flower, be sure to collect the seeds, as the plants usually die shortly after.

You can identify this species by its flower scape, which is glandular. The flowers are white to pink with multiple flowers occurring on a single scape, which is typical of Florida sundews. Flowers occur in the spring and may carry on throughout a warm, wet summer. They produce a lot of seeds, which can help you populate your bog. Compared to *D. capillaris*, the leaves are more wedge, triangular, or spoon shaped. When grown in full sun, they are a dark bronze to blood-red compared to *D. capillaris*.

Drosera brevifolia. JOHN BRUEGGEN

Drosera brevifolia.

DROSERA CAPILLARIS—
PINK SUNDEW

Like *D. brevifolia*, *D. capillaris* is a small, low-lying sundew but with rounded traps. Found in wiregrasses along with other species of carnivorous plants, this very common sundew is a little gem. Its variants range from decumbent and chubby in central Alabama to erect and long in central Florida.

Drosera capillaris 'Long Arm'.
JIM SCOTT STRAUS

Drosera capillaris.

DROSERA FILIFORMIS VAR. FLORIDANA—THREADLEAF SUNDEW

Drosera filiformis var. *floridana*'s range is limited to Florida. It has narrower, shorter leaves that are orange, red, or purple compared to the North Atlantic's greener and larger *Drosera filiformis* var. *filiformis*. The Florida variant also has thinner, shorter scapes and smaller flowers. Barry Rice chose the varietal epithet *floridana* instead of subspecies since the population could experience gene flow due to migratory birds moving north and south.

When this plant is found within the same area as *D. capillaris* or *Drosera brevifolia*, it is believed that the pollinators going to *Drosera filiformis* are too large for the smaller species and therefore reduce the chance of cross-pollinating. Found in Bay and predominantly Washington counties, they grow in sandy locations along shallow waterways.

Drosera filiformis var. *floridana*.

Drosera filiformis var. *floridana*. MANNY HERRERA

79

DROSERA INTERMEDIA—WATER SUNDEW, OBLONG-LEAVED SUNDEW, SPOONLEAF SUNDEW, SPATULATE-LEAVED SUNDEW

D. intermedia can be found in Europe, Canada, and the United States. There it grows as a temperate species. Plants found in central Florida go dormant. Often seen in inundated margins, some specimens can be seen growing in dense mats on the surface of the water! Often seen in inundated margins, some specimens can be seen growing in dense mats on the surface of the water! Florida's tropical form has smaller rosettes of leaves compared to those found in the north.

After it emerges from its **hibernacula** in the spring, it will grow until late fall. The flowers appear from June to August and are usually white with a hint of pink. Plantlets forming on the flower spike is common with this species. This phenomenon is known as **apomixis**.

D. ×hybrida is a naturally occurring New Jersey hybrid between *Drosera filiformis* and *Drosera intermedia*. The characteristics are a mix of the two species, resulting in long leaves with blunt tips. It grows well in a variety of conditions.

Drosera intermedia.

Drosera intermedia. JIM FOWLER

DROSERA TRACYI—TRACY'S OR GULF COAST THREADLEAF SUNDEW

Drosera tracyi is closely related to *Drosera fili-formis*. *Drosera tracyi* ranges from the Gulf coast of Louisiana to the Florida Panhandle and into southern Georgia. Its flowers do not self-pollinate easily, and hybrids between them and *Drosera filiformis* are known as *Drosera* 'California Sunset' due to an artificial hybrid made in California. Hybrids between *Drosera filiformis* var. *floridana* ×*tracyi* are known as *D.* ×*californica* var. *arenaria* even though it is a natural hybrid found in a small lake in Washington County, Florida. *D.* ×*californica* var. *arenaria* is large like its *Drosera tracyi* parent but red like the *Drosera filiformis* var. *floridana* parent.

Drosera tracyi.

Drosera tracyi flower. JOHN BRUEGGEN

Drosera tracyi, Liberty County, Florida.
MANNY HERRERA

81

Florida's Drosera Dichotomous Key

1	Leaf blades filiform (threadlike)	>2
1	Leaf blades linear, round, elongate-spatulate, or **cuneate**	>3
2	Glandular trichomes orange, red, or reddish-purple	*Drosera filiformis* var. *floridana*
2	Glandular trichomes pale green	*Drosera tracyi*
3	Glandular scapes; **stipules** absent or reduced to minute hairs; seeds crater-shaped and black	*Drosera brevifolia*
3	Stipules free from **petioles** or essentially so	>4
4	Plants always arranged in a rosette; petioles flat, petals usually pink	*Drosera capillaris*
4	Plants rosulate when young, developing leafy stems 1–8 cm; petioles filiform, glabrous; petals white, seeds uniformly **papillose**	*Drosera intermedia*

Commonly cared-for carnivores. Look for these to add to your collection.

Drosera capillaris.

Drosera intermida. ALEX ROUKIS

Drosera filiformis.

Powdery Strap Air Plant

Of the 2,500 bromeliads in the world, sixteen of them are native to Florida. Like all bromeliads, this carnivorous one looks like the top of a pineapple. Three bromeliads have been classified as carnivorous so far, the other two being not native to Florida (*Brocchina reducta, B. tatei*). While many bromeliads use detritus for nutrition, *Catopsis berteroniana* grows as an epiphyte attached to trees out in full sun away from the canopy. It uses its roots to anchor to trees and does not obtain nutrients from its host. Endangered in Florida, it can be found in thin trees like buttonwoods and mangroves alongside the highway of the Everglades National Park in Collier, Dade, and Monroe counties. Their habitat can range from rockland hammocks to sloughs or tidal swamps, but they are usually found on high branches. They flower year-round, most notably in the fall through winter.

Its South American name, *lampera de la selva* (jungle lantern), is derived from its appearance in the bright sunlight. *C. berteroniana* looks more yellow than green due to the high-intensity light of the open canopy. Its chalky powder amplifies this lantern look. Many carnivorous plants have a wax coating to aid in trapping their victims. The slippery surface causes insects to slip. The powder also reflects ultraviolet light, causing insects to collide with the leaf and fall into the tank.

When its tanks are inspected, they contain many more terrestrial arthropods than the average bromeliad, causing scientists to classify them as carnivorous. Like *Sarracenia, C. berteroniana* provides a microhabitat for many inquilines. The **phytotelmata** can provide homes for nearly a dozen types of larva, including *Wyeomyia mitchellii*. This species of mosquito takes two weeks to develop inside the tank. During this time, it has a mutualistic relationship with the plant. The carnivorous bromeliad provides a home for the larvae, and the larvae break down the caught insects, which aids in the plant's digestion.

While *C. berteroniana* is endangered in Florida, it is doing better in the West Indies, Mexico, Central America, and South America. Threats in Florida include poaching, habitat loss, and the invasive Mexican bromeliad weevil. This evil weevil (*Metamasius callizona*) came into Florida in 1989 through a nursery in Broward County. By the time they discovered it, it had spread and infected native bromeliads. In two years, it had moved to four Florida counties, and by 1999 it had infected plants in sixteen counties. The weevils lay eggs in the largest, most mature bromeliads, where their larvae eat the stems, killing the plant. Since the weevil concentrates on large plants, it is taking out many plants that are mature enough to reproduce. Eleven of the sixteen species of native bromeliads are under attack by this invasive weevil. In addition to the weevil, *C. berteroniana* has to combat invasive plant species like air potato (*Dioscorea bulbifera*) and Japanese climbing fern (*Lygodium japonicum*). Current estimates of controlling Florida's invasive plants are estimated at $100 million each year, which does not include the management of invasive animals.

The endangered carnivorous bromeliad *Catopsis berteroniana*. CELINE LEROY

Catopsis berteroniana.

While uncommon in cultivation in the United States, tissue cultures of *C. berteroniana* are rarely available from European distributors. If you are looking for a carnivorous bromeliad to add to your collection, try *B. reducta*.

Catopsis berteroniana. CELINE LEROY

Conservation

"Conservation is a state of harmony between men and land."
—Aldo Leopold, American conservationist, 1949

Knowing the conservation threats for each of the Florida carnivorous plant genera will help guide policy makers on how to prioritize funding for endangered species and how to prevent threats for others. Only 3 percent of the 268,000 species of flowering plants have been evaluated by the International Union for the Conservation of Nature. Of that small group studied, 70 percent have been listed as threatened (i.e., vulnerable, endangered, or critically endangered). That is not a good track record. In that subgroup, many are carnivorous plant species.

While carnivorous plants can be found on six continents in a range of different habitats, many share the same threats of agriculture, deforestation, drainage, eutrophication, and fire suppression.

Biggest Threats Genera Face Globally Today

Drosera	Agricultural activities
Sarracenia	Natural system modifications, invasive species, pollution, overcollection, agriculture
Utricularia	Pollution

According to a recent Harvard study, the most common threat for carnivorous plants has to do with agriculture. The direct habitat loss from planting crops for humans and for grazing animals is detrimental to carnivorous plants. It is estimated by the United Nations that by 2050 the human population will increase by 33 percent to 9.6 billion people. Meat and milk production are also expected to increase. As of the time of writing this, only 55 percent of the world's crops are fed to humans. These crops are thirsty, accounting for 70 percent of the global water usage. The remaining 45 percent of the crops produced are fed primarily to livestock or turned into biofuels. Eating the crops directly and bypassing the livestock seems like one viable option to reduce the need for crop land. This is especially true of land animals that need higher feed-to-meat ratios than aquatic animals.

Another possible solution is to figure out the food waste and food loss problem, which accounts for around one-third of all food produced. While some food is thrown away due to spoilage, a lot of it gets sent to the dump due to superficial cosmetic reasons. When I taught agriculture, I would ask my students, "If you walked out of the grocery store with three bags and dropped one, would you keep walking or go back and pick it up?" Wasting food is not just about money. It's also about the water, energy, space, and time needed to produce it. According to Feeding America, in Florida 2.7 million people struggle with food security, which includes one in five children. While it will require a herculean effort, this agriculture and habitat loss problem seems like something that humanity could come up with several solutions to.

The second biggest threat to carnivorous plants is biological resource use. This includes the collection of wild plants and activities like logging, which also result in direct habitat loss. In addition to removing plants from their natural habitat, a consequent problem is that collectors usually remove the most mature and largest specimens. Since carnivorous plants are slow to develop, the constant loss of older individuals severely impacts the population because it prevents reproduction. Another problem is that collectors are choosing the more rare or atypical plants, leading to less biodiversity. Genetic diversity is crucial for a species' longevity, especially in a changing environment. According to the Harvard study, collection of wild plants was particularly common to *Sarracenia* as well as non-Florida species like *Darlingtonia*, *Nepenthes*, and Venus flytraps, although I have also read that Venus flytraps are at such low populations in the Carolinas that poaching is not really a problem because there are not enough left to poach. While doing research for this book, I read several sources published in the past twenty years that provided recommendations on how to field collect. Field collecting can be tempting, but it is most likely illegal—be ethical and do not do it. I see no rationale for digging up wild plants. There are many universities, biological research stations, and organizations that with government approval can better relocate, propagate, and research compared to a backyard hobbyist.

Collection of wild plants is a major threat to *Sarracenia* species like this *Sarracenia alabamensis* subsp. *wherryi*.
ALAN CRESSLER

86

Tragedy of the Commons

Collecting specimens in the field or poaching, depending on your angle, reminds me of the shared-resource situation called tragedy of the commons. I learned about this concept in my global sustainability master's degree. It describes how individuals act independently in their own self-interest and thus tend to overexploit resources. The original example involved farmers allowing their sheep to graze on shared public or common land. Farmers wanted to make more money, so they added sheep to the commons. But because all farmers want to increase their profits and so all introduced more sheep, the land was quickly pushed beyond its carrying capacity. The degradation of resources negatively affects everyone. Today this concept can be applied to a multitude of finite resources we share on Earth. If I were to walk on a boardwalk in a park and remove the carnivorous plants, I would not just be depleting the enjoyment for the next family; I would be ruining a key player in the Florida ecosystem.

Pollution, including urban waste, fertilizer and pesticide run-off, and industrial pollutants, is the third most common threat to carnivorous plants. Herbicides can kill carnivorous plants directly, while fertilizers can cause eutrophication events. Excessive nutrients in bodies of water alter the natural food chain and make the habitat for carnivorous plants unlivable. Alternatively, these nutrient-adding events can make it more favorable for other plants and can cause algae blooms like red tide. Specifically, *Utricularia purpurea* populations have declined due to agriculture-associated eutrophication. David Jennings of the University of South Florida found that insecticide use above, within, and below the recommended treatment level can be harmful to carnivorous plants. While it may be easy to blame Big Ag, Florida Master Gardeners are quick to point out that residents misuse grass fertilizers much more than commercial agriculture.

The fourth most common threat to carnivorous plants is modification of natural systems. These changes include fire suppression, water management, and draining, all of which are intended to improve human quality of life. Governments say we must suppress fires to save homes that are encroaching on forests. Water is drained from wetlands to create habitable real estate for housing developments. Wetlands are also drained to create additional farmland, where this water is then reintroduced for irrigation.

Of the ten professors I encountered during my master's in global sustainability, only one was brave enough to talk about the impact of a growing human population. An increasing population, especially an exponential one, has a huge environmental impact. Reducing population growth would have noticeable positive climate-related effects. One major factor is the way we currently eat. We currently waste one-third of all food produced, some of which is only due to aesthetic preferences. If we could reduce our population growth, we would need to do less modification of the natural systems. We could focus on saving food and redirecting it to the currently poverty-stricken population. Population growth is a delicate and nuanced subject and unfortunately beyond the scope of this project. It would be remarkable if couples considered the environment and the Earth's finite resources in their family planning.

While those threats posed to carnivorous plants may seem unrelated, the best chance for the

Drosera filiformis var. *floridana*. MANNY HERRERA

plants (and us) is to approach the problems in a holistic manner. Carnivorous plant conservation is unique in that they face different challenges compared to other taxa. Habitats in which carnivorous plants live are often within larger ecosystems. These microhabitats can be dissociated from larger climatic patterns.

For example, while the local region may be experiencing a seasonal drought, the waterlogged habitat of carnivorous plants may not be experiencing the same pressures. Another tricky aspect of conserving carnivorous plants is that they tend to have small, fragmented ranges with specific habitat needs, while some species may be cosmopolitan with a small population size. This leads to each genus and possibly each species needing its own preservation plan.

WHO CARES?

American conservationist Aldo Leopold once wrote, "There are some who can live without wild things, and some who cannot." Today we know that in fact we *all* need wild things and a functioning ecosystem to support our life.

Healthy ecosystems are resilient. As logging and habitat destruction occurs around the world, humans need to go deeper into the tropical forests to access resources. This is increasing our exposure to wild animals and the pathogens they may carry. Reducing habitats is also causing wildlife to leave their forests, which adds to the chance they will interact with domestic animals, which can also increase disease transmission.

There was a misunderstanding that nature was resetting from years of human activity during the COVID-19 pandemic. Dolphins did not return to the canals of Venice, and critically endangered animals did not reclaim city streets. While there was less air and car travel, diesel-burning trucks made up for it by delivering more packages to individual homes.

What does any of this have to do with carnivorous plants? Conserving carnivorous plants could also benefit other species. There are complex and surprising interdependencies between carnivorous plants and other species. It's not just that carnivorous plants eat animals; some species provide homes for plants and animals. Pitcher plant species around the world provide habitats for entire communities. These organisms are specialists and rely on the pitcher plants. We should want to save carnivorous plants because their loss could also result in secondary extinctions.

For those with a more **speciesist** mindset, carnivorous plants provide humans with information, medicine, and pest and disease control. While a collection of them at your home may not act as a reliable form of pest control, wild populations when in full residence consume large quantities of dipterans. These insects, which include mosquitoes, midges, deerflies, and horseflies, are not only annoying but can transmit diseases to humans. *Utricularia* species predate on mosquito eggs and larvae and even eat the parasitic flatworm that gives humans schistosomiasis. While not in the United States, this disease is only second to malaria as the most destructive parasitic disease.

Carnivorous plants have a lot to teach us. *Nepenthes* are inspiring scientists around the world to create bioinspired materials that could be used for self-cleaning windows, frictionless blood transfusions, therapeutic treatments, and biocontrol solutions in agriculture. Sundews' glue is helping with medical suturing. What else can these plants teach us? We have to save them to find out.

Cultivation's Role in Conservation

As a student of science, you have great responsibility. Now that you know the wonderous world of carnivorous plants, you will likely want to save their wild siblings and their habitats. You can help wild plants, especially endangered ones, by growing plants that are only grown legally. Luckily, today most carnivorous plants that are for sale have been produced in backyards, nurseries, and laboratories lawfully. Horticulturists and hobbyists work hard on artificially selected specimens to obtain colorful plants with special patterns and traits. Growers trade pollen and seeds through the mail. These plants are usually more colorful and robust than their wild counterparts. Using micropropagation, rare specimens can be cloned into thousands of individuals.

Carnivorous plants are no longer just for geeky introverts. Today half of hobbyists are female. From memes to movies, people are celebrating these unique plants. Decals, stickers, and T-shirts honor these predatory plants. Carnivorous plants are being appreciated not just because they are carnivorous but also because they are beautiful.

Passionate hobbyists and naturalists must take action to ensure sites are secured and protected so we can continue to celebrate carnivorous plants and learn from them or else we will be met with road-widening projects, car dealerships, and housing developments.

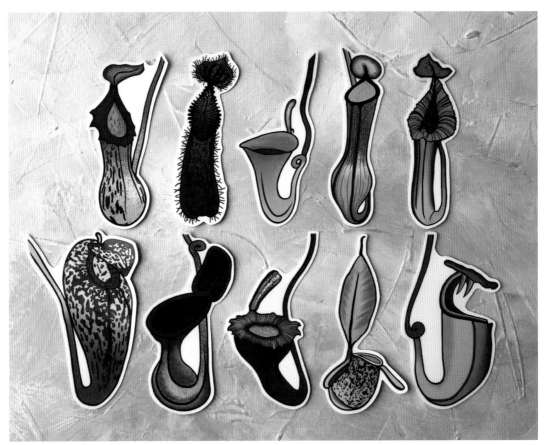

Check out these beautiful decals. LINDSAY BONNETT OF NEPENTHES DESIGNS

89

Micropropagation and Tissue Culture

Tissue culturing is a method in which small pieces of a plant (**explant**) are introduced into an artificial nutrient-dense medium. Tissue culture is the first step in micropropagation. Following are the steps involved in micropropagation:

Stage I Establishment
Stage II Multiplication
Stage III Rooting
Stage IV Acclimatization

The use of micropropagation to help in conservation efforts is exciting. Currently, projects from around the world are using micropropagation to propagate and consequently conserve rare and endangered plant species. From one piece, thousands of mature plants can be created.

Following are some ways you can enjoy carnivorous plants while helping protect and conserve them:

1. **Buy from trustworthy nurseries only.** It's easy and cheap to order plants from reputable online sources and established nurseries. Don't take plants from the wild or support nurseries that do. For many of the genera discussed in this book, human-made hybrids are more colorful and robust than their wild counterparts. If you want a specific species, ask the grower for pictures of all the plants. Poached plants vary greatly in size and may have weeds, sand, and gravel mixed in the growing medium. Nursery-grown plants are usually similar in size and are grown in a weed-free peat moss medium.

2. **Educate others about the value of wild habitats.** If the rainforests are the lungs of the Earth, then the wetlands and swamps are the kidneys. The soils that are created in wetlands store carbon for hundreds of years and help combat climate change. Wetlands provide homes to a large portion of threatened and endangered organisms. These ecosystems improve our water quality, help prevent flooding and shoreline erosion, and provide unique opportunities for recreation.

3. **Join and support the North American Sarracenia Conservancy (NASC).** The NASC is a nonprofit organization dedicated to preserving the natural habitats and genetic diversity of the genus *Sarracenia*.

4. **Join the International Carnivorous Plant Society (ICPS).** The ICPS is an organization of horticulturists, conservationists, scientists, and educators all interested in sharing knowledge and news of carnivorous plants. As a member you'll receive a quarterly newsletter with exciting new research and growing tips.

5. **Join, support, and volunteer with your local conservation organizations.** Contemplate what American philosopher William James said: "Act as if what you do makes a difference. It does." I am reminded of humorist David Sedaris, who was so repulsed by the litter problem in his town that he began spending three to eight hours each day picking up trash. Voluntarily.

6. **Plant native plants in your yard.** Join your local native plant society, like your area's version of the Florida Native Plant Society. They'll be able to help you transform your yard into a wildlife-attracting, aesthetically pleasing Florida oasis.

7. **Propagate your plants, and share with friends.** By sharing and selling your plants, the need for others to collect from the wild will decrease. And it's fun to share.

8. **Reduce your carbon footprint.** Refuse one-time paper and plastic materials, reduce what you purchase, reuse what you can, rot kitchen scraps in a composting bin, and, as a last step, recycle. Recycling takes a lot of energy and resources.

9. **Remove invasive species from your yard.** Learn how to identify common backyard invaders and remove them appropriately. Many times, governments suggest *not* placing them in the yard waste container, as the compost may not reach high enough temperatures to neutralize these invasive plants. Put them directly in the trash.

10. **Support sustainable florists.** Patronize shops that do not use *Sarracenia* pitchers in their flower arrangements. Most pitchers are collected from wild plants, which decreases the chance of the plants catching their next meal. If you grow a lot of *Sarracenia*, talk to your local florist about your surplus pitchers in the fall—they'll most likely welcome the unique leaves.

11. **Take only pictures and leave the pitchers.** Stay on marked paths when you visit the homes of wild carnivorous plants. If you are lucky enough to discover a new patch of carnivorous plants, don't advertise their location. Poachers are on social media too and can use your image to get the exact GPS coordinates—which is both scary and sad.

12. **Vote.** Support businesses and legislators that protect the environment. Florida's carnivorous plants are special. Find companies and lawmakers that value the protection of a range of habitats like bogs, lakes, forests, and wetlands. We shouldn't be draining the swamp!

Sybilline Books

At the end of *Last Chance to See* by authors Douglas Adams and Mark Carwardine, they highlight the story of the Sybilline books. Their book is about globetrotting to see the rarest of the rare animal species before they go extinct. Its connection to the Sybilline story was so powerful I wanted to share it here with my own updated version to highlight today's environmental, social, and economic crises.

In the recent past there was a large and prosperous population in the middle of a great cosmos. The denizens saw plenty of newcomers visiting on their way from the great metropolises that existed outside the horizon. They saw human-made items as aesthetically pleasing and wilderness as too sunny, too windy, and too insect-ridden. No one followed an austere lifestyle.

The townspeople lived in excess and had many luxuries. Verdant lawns grew inedible vegetation and flanked congested roads. These grid-locked roads held carbon-dioxide-emitting vehicles that were spacious yet contained only single individuals. The tires of these vehicles left chemicals on the road, which washed into the waterways. But the waterways traveled outward from the town, and no one was alarmed. Vacant buildings illuminated fluorescent lights day and night. Citizens had disdain for those who favored a plant-based diet. They loved red meat. The more they ate, the greater their status. Wet areas were drained, and water was reallocated to stop naturally occurring fires. Monoculture grasses grew where species-rich habitats used to flourish. The elite putt balls into holes as a pastime.

One day, a weathered crone approached the town's border. She brought with her a canvas bag full of nine sand-covered tablets.

"All the knowledge and wisdom of the world," she advertised. "Only one sack of gold." It was a small sacrifice for the town. The people laughed at the old woman. They thought she must not be very wise to sell so many books for such a trivial price. They thought she did not understand what was truly valuable.

As the sun lowered, the woman purchased a small pile of firewood and created a bonfire. She burned five books to lessen her burden as she returned home. All the knowledge and wisdom of the world is a heavy load to bear.

An entire year came and went. The town's resources teetered but remained generally stable. A few people became ill, but it did not affect the majority of people directly, so most went about their normal routines of consumption and gluttony.

Off in the distance, they saw the old woman approaching the town slowly yet purposefully. Not again, the townspeople thought.

"Four books that contain all the knowledge and wisdom of the world," she advertised. "This time the price has changed."

The townspeople shrugged her off. Not impressed by her arrival, they carried on with their leisurely day.

"Four books," she repeated. A few townspeople who had been directly affected by the illness in their own families approached her.

"How much?" they asked.

"Two bars of gold," she said.

"What?" they exclaimed. As they questioned this woman's intelligence, more townspeople gathered. With the crowd growing, the porcine town leader came out and told the woman that they were not interested. They were not about to pay double for less than half of the original product. That wasn't a deal.

The woman purchased a small amount of firewood and built another bonfire. She then burned two more books. She was aging, and the tablets were heavy. The next morning, the original people who were interested in the knowledge sifted through the embers. Sadly, it was only ashes. They were too late.

Another year passed, and this time more people became ill, including those who grew, processed, and transported the food. The illness was spreading. It didn't discriminate, even affecting the leader for a short time. Many resources were diverted to be used in his recovery—many resources that were not available to the general populace. In addition to the disease, the climate was changing rapidly. Staple crops were not able to adapt.

As the old woman approached the town on her annual pilgrimage, the leader greeted her personally. "Welcome back," he bellowed with excitement. "You're early."

"The trip was easier," she said as she opened her bag, showing the two remaining books.

"How much?" the leader grunted, in hopes of appeasing his citizens.

"Four bars of gold," she said.

"That's too much. You're crazy and ugly and horse-faced. We are having a *little* trouble this year. We can't afford it."

"Firewood. Please."

They refused, so she lit one of the books on fire. It burned fine by itself. She left with the final book.

The following year, when the woman returned, the town was in desperate shape. With their original wild west mentality, they had extracted and altered the natural resources so drastically that they couldn't get out of their current situation. Their resources were finite, yet their economy was built on infinite greed. The soil was so degraded and eroded that they couldn't amend it. Pollutants had infected the wilderness so significantly, like the pandemic had infected them, that it was hard to envision the next chapter of their civilization.

The woman held the last book in her skeletal hand. "It contains one-ninth of the knowledge and wisdom of the world, and it is extremely valuable."

"The price?" the townspeople asked as the leader stewed in his white castle.

"Eight bricks of gold."

"We understand," they sighed. And the townspeople exchanged all their remaining gold for a single tablet. "It better be worth it," they added.

"It is," the woman replied. "You should have seen the rest of it."

Growing Guide

Here is a concise guide to growing Florida's carnivorous plants. Carnivorous plants from around the world do best with pure water. Use reverse-osmosis, distilled, or rainwater. Outdoor plants do not require fertilizers but may benefit from them. MaxSea 16-16-16 can be used on many carnivorous plants 1–2 times a month at ¼ tsp per gallon. Hand feeding tiny organisms to your plants can also be beneficial and exciting!

Use this chart as what it is—a guide. A friend in Lake Wales, Florida must provide shade for her Venus flytraps in the summer, while I need to give them as much light as possible due to the oaks that grow south of their setup. One of my favorite things to do is to experiment.

I have found growing carnivorous plants to be beneficial for my mental, social, and physical health. I look forward to checking in with them every morning. I hope by growing Florida's native carnivorous plant species you cultivate a bog, knowledge, and friendship. I certainly have.

	Bladderworts *Utricularia sp.* Nicknames: *Utrics*	Butterworts *Pinguicula sp.* Nicknames: *Pings*
Dormancy	May stop flowering in colder months, but do not require a true dormancy.	Do not require dormancy and should be protected from frost to maintain growing year-round.
Habitat Range	Found throughout Florida	Found throughout Florida
Indoors	Aquatic and terrestrial species can be kept indoors but will require a grow light.	Do not do well indoors.
Light	Full sun	Part to full sun
Pots	3-inch plastic or glazed pots for one mature clump of terrestrial species. For aquatic species, the larger the container the more the conditions will be buffered. While I have started small species in glass jars, they do best in 1-gallon vessels, while larger species require small ponds or large aquariums averaging 50 gallons or more.	4–6 inch plastic or glazed pots with drainage for one adult plant. Wider pots allow some species, like *P. primuliflora* to pup out easier. If kept in undrained pots do not inundate.
Soil	Terrestrial plants can be kept in a rough continuum of one part sphagnum peat moss to one part sand.	Equal parts play sand and sphagnum peat moss. Combinations of peat, sand and perlite are also suitable.
Water	For terrestrial species use the tray method. For aquatic species use pond water with peat moss added as a substrate to reduce algae growth. Aquatic *Utricularia* do well with other aquatic plants which help maintain the water parameters.	Use tray method, keeping damp to wet throughout the year.

North American Pitcher Plants	Sundews	Venus Flytrap
Sarracenia sp. Nicknames: *Trumpet Plant, Pitcher Plant, Dumb Watches*	*Drosera sp.*	*Dionaea muscipula* Nicknames: *Flytraps, Meadow Clam, Tippitiwitchet, VFT*
All require cool temperatures and reduction in light from Thanksgiving to Valentine's day allows them to recharge.	Three of our Florida species (excluding *D. brevifolia* and *D. capillaris*) produce hibernacula in winter.	If grown outside, plants will slow down in winter. If kept inside, maintain a 12–16 hour photoperiod and feed often to keep plants healthy.
Sarracenia species found on the East coast of North America from Canada to mid Florida.	Found throughout Florida	15 counties in North Carolina and 1 county in South Carolina. Allochthonous population in Liberty County, Florida.
S. rosea could be kept indoors with a grow light. Would still require a dormancy period. Do best outdoors.	Will require grow lights, or a brightly lit South facing window.	They can be kept indoors, but only if given a grow light.
Full sun	Full sun	12–16 bright, direct sun/grow lights during the growing season.
8-inch plastic or glazed pot for one mature plant. Move them up to larger pots slowly. They can be divided and transplanted every 3–5 years.	3-inch plastic or glazed pots with drainage for one adult plant.	5-inch plastic or glazed pot for one mature plant. VFTs do best when transplanted into a fresh substrate every 1–2 years to prevent soil from accumulating salts and minerals.
All sphagnum peat moss, or equal parts sphagnum peat moss and sand.	Plants can be kept in a rough continuum of one part sphagnum peat moss to one part sand. Can also be grown in 100% sphagnum moss.	Plants can be kept in a rough continuum of one part sphagnum peat moss to one part sand. Can also be grown in 100% sphagnum moss.
Keep a dish underneath the pot to keep soil very damp. Have them sit in 1 inch of water during the growing season and less during dormancy.	Use tray method, keeping damp to wet throughout the year.	Keep a shallow dish underneath the pot to keep soil damp in the winter months and wet in the summer. Plants should only sit in a little bit of water. Even though they do best wet, VFTs are usually found in areas with low water tables. For plants grown indoors keep the soil damp year round.

Glossary

adaptation—an inherited trait that helps an organism live and reproduce in its environment.

ala—vertical extension/wing/fin that runs down the front of a pitcher.

allochthonous—originating in a place other than where it is found.

apomixis—a form of asexual reproduction that involves vegetative bulbils or buds being produced in the inflorescence instead of flowers.

areolae—circular, chlorophyll-free patches that light can penetrate.

autonym—used in trinomial nomenclature when species and subspecies/variety names are the same.

basionym—original name on which a new name is based.

cleistogamy—self-fertilization that occurs within a permanently closed flower.

corolla—the petals of a flower, considered as a unit.

cuneate—obtriangular or wedge-shaped.

decumbent—lying along the ground or along a surface, with the extremity curving upward.

dome swamp—an isolated, forested, depression wetland occurring within a fire-maintained community.

ecotone—a region of transition between two biological communities.

elliptic—oval in outline and with a length:breadth ration between 3:2 and 2:1.

epibionts—an organism that lives on the surface of another living organism.

etiolated—feeble, pale, and drawn out due to a lack of light.

evolutionarily significant unit (ESU)—a population of organisms that is considered distinct for purposes of conservation.

explant—a cell, organ, or piece of tissue that is transferred from an organism to a nutrient medium.

extirpated—a species that no longer exists in a specific region.

fimbriate—tooth- or feather-edged.

floriferous—produces many flowers.

galeate—being in the shape of a helmet; helmet-shaped.

hammock—stands of trees, usually hardwood, that form an ecological island.

heterosis—another term for hybrid vigor; traits are enhanced as a result of mixing the genetic contributions of its parents.

hibernacula—Latin for "tent for winter quarters." In botany refers to various winter buds. In zoology could reference hives, pods, cocoons, and subterranean burrows that help an organism survive winter.

hydrophobic—tending to repel or fail to mix with water.

inquiline—an animal exploiting the living space of another.

mesic—containing a moderate amount of moisture, wet.

nastic—a movement of plant parts that is independent of the direction of the external stimulus.

nothospecies—a hybrid that is formed by hybridization of two species, not other hybrids.

obovate—similar to ovate but attached at the narrower end and with a length:breadth ratio between 3:2 and 2:1.

ovate—resembling a section through the long axis of an egg, attached near the broader end and with a length:breadth ration between 3:2 and 2:1.

palate—cylindrical structure protruding from flower center.

papillose—pimply; a surface covered with raised dots or pimples.

peduncle—the stalk bearing a flower or fruit, or the main stalk of an inflorescence.

petioles—the stalk that joins a leaf to a stem.

phenotype—observable/physical characteristics of an individual.

phytotelma (plural phytotelmata)—a water-filled cavity in a terrestrial plant that may serve as the habitat for a variety of organisms.

plug—immature plants raised in small, individual cells, ready to be transplanted into containers or a garden.

polymorphic—genetic variation resulting in several different forms or types of individuals within a single species.

raceme—unbranched indeterminate inflorescence in which the flowers are arranged along a single central axis.

revolute—rolled backward or downward.

rugulose—finely wrinkled.

saccate—pouched.

sessile—attached directly by its base without a stalk or peduncle.

speciesist—treating members of one species as superior to members of other species.

stipules—a small leaflike appendage to a leaf, typically borne in pairs at the base of the leaf stalk.

subreniform—shaped slightly like the human kidney.

transverse—broader than long.

trichome—small, hair-like growths found on plants.

trullate—resembling a trowel blade.

turions—a wintering bud that is capable of growing into a complete plant.

Index

aquatic, 27, 49, 57, 59, 60, 61, 66, 85, 96

Banks, Joseph, 17
bladderworts (*Utricularia*), 1, 57–67, 96
bog garden, 23, 28, 50, 60, 71
bromeliad, 5, 11, *11*, 83–84, *83*, *84*
Broward, Napoleon Bonaparte, *15*, 15
butterworts (*Pinguicula*), 12, 27, 69–76, 96

carnivorous plants, ix, 1–30, *3*, *21*, 85–88
    dormancy, 4, *5*, 5, 26, 27, 96
    feeding, 1, 5, 35, 95, 97
    fertilizer, 26, 87, 95
Catopsis berteronian, *2*, 11, *11*, 83–84, *83*, *84*
Chen, Maggie, *33*, 33
Cohn, Ferdinand, 58
conservation, 8, 15, 16, *33*, 70, 85–91
containers, 21–24, *21*, *24*, 74, 96
cultivars, 3, 6, 39, 47, 51
cultivation, 39, 44, 53, 57, 59, 61, 64, 74, 78, 84, 89–91

Darwin, Charles, vii, 17, 18, 33, 58, 59
Dionaea muscipula, 6, 17, *34*, 97.
    See also venus flytrap
disease(s), 1, 88, 93
dormancy, 4, *5*, *5*, 26, 27, 96–97
Douglas, Marjory Stoneman, 14, 16, *16*, 17
Drosera (sundews), *2*, 7, 11, *22*, 24, 26, 27, 58, 77–82, *77*, 85, *87*, 97
Drosera brevifolia, 78, *78*, 82, 97
Drosera capillaris, 78, *78*, 82, *82*, 97
Drosera filiformis var. *floridana*, *2*, *77*, 79, *79*, 82, *87*
Drosera intermedia, *2*, 80, *80*, 82, *82*
Drosera tracyi, 81, *81*, 82

Eilts, Alex, 11, 12
Everglades, 11, 14–16, *14*, 17, 18, 83
evolution, 1, 5–6
evolutionarily significant unit (ESU), 8

fertilizers, 26, 87

Gonella, Paulo, 77
greenhouse(s), 26, 27, 64

habitats, 1, 8, 12, 13, 18, 31, 42, 43, 46, 49, 61, 62, 66, 70, 71–72, 77, 83, 85–88, 89, 90, 91, 96–97
    See also individual plants
Hedrich, Rainer, 31

hooded pitcher plant, 47, 48.
    See also Sarracenia minor
Hooker, Joseph, 58

infusoria, 59
International Carnivorous Plant Society, ix, 90

Jennings, May Mann, 15, *15*

Kew Botanical Gardens, 17, *18*, *51*, 58

Leopold, Aldo, 85, 88
light, 1, 5, 23, 24, 26, 27, 32, 33, 49, 50, 53, 60, 61, 69, 70, 71, 73, 74, 83, 95, 96–97
Linnaeus, Carl, 6, 17

Merian, Maria Sibylla, 17
micropropagation, 3, 89–90

North American pitcher plants (*Sarracenia*), 1, 4, 6, 39–56, 97

parrot pitcher plant, 7, 8, 49.
    See also Sarracenia psittacina
peat moss, 23, 24, 28, 90, 96–97
perlite, 23, 24, 28, 96
pesticides, 28, 87
pests, 1, 27–28, 29
Pinguicula (butterworts), 11, 12, *13*, 26, 27, 29, 58, 69–76, *69*, *70*, *71*, *72*, *73*, *74*, *75*, *76*, 96
Pinguicula caerulea, 71, *71*, 76
Pinguicula ionantha, 69, 70, 71, *71*
Pinguicula lutea, 69, 70, 72, *72*, 76
Pinguicula planifolia, 69, *69*, 70, *70*, 73, *73*, 76
Pinguicula primuliflora, 74, *74*, 76, 96
Pinguicula pumila, *13*, 75, *75*
powdery strap air plant, 83–84
propagate, 3, 24, 34, 40, 57, 72, 74, 86, 90

Rice, Barry, 79

Sarracenia (North American pitcher plants), 4, 5, *7*, *7*, 8, *8*, 11, *12*, *18*, *19*, 22, *23*, 24, *24*, 26, *26*, 27, *27*, 29, 39–56, *39*, *42*, *43*, *44*, *47*, *48*, *50*, *51*, *52*, *54*, *55*, *56*, 57, 58, 64, 83, 85, 86, *86*, 90, 97
Sarracenia, habitat, 43, 45, 46, 48, 49, 52, 54
Sarracenia Northwest, *23*, 24, *24*
Sarracenia flava, 8, *18*, 26, *27*, 40, 41, 42, 44, *44*, 45, 46, 51, 54
Sarracenia leucophylla, *19*, *24*, 26, 40, 42, 46, *47*, 50, 54, *55*

Sarracenia minor, *12*, 39, 40, 47, *47*, 48, *48*, 54
Sarracenia psittacina, 7, *7*, 8, 40, 47, 49, 50, *50*, 54
Sarracenia rosea, 27, *39*, 40, *41*, 50–52, *51*, *52*, 54, *55*, 97
Sarracenia rubra subsp. *gulfensis*, 8, *26*, 40, 53–54, *53*
Sarracenia rubra subsp. *wherryi*, 8, 43, 54, *86*
Sarrazin, M. S., 39
slugs, 27
snails, 27
soil, 1, 19, 21, 22, 23, 24, 28, 90, 96–97
Sowerby, James, 57
sphagnum moss, 23, 24, 28, 33, 53, 74, 96–97
sphagnum peat moss, 28, 96–97
Stoneman, Frank, 15–16
sundews (*Drosera*), 1, 5, 22, 23, 26, 27, 77–82, 88, 97

terrariums, 33, 64, 69
terrestrial, 1, 27, 49, 57, 59, 64, 66–67, 83, 96
threadleaf sundew, 79, 81
tissue culture, 39, 47, 50, 51, 84, 90
Treat, Mary, 58

Utricularia (bladderworts), *3*, 5, 11, 23, 27, 29, 57–67, *57*, *58*, *59*, *60*, *61*, *62*, *63*, *64*, 85, 87, 88, 96
Utricularia, aquatic, 27, 57, 59, 96
Utricularia, terrestrial, 27, 57
Utricularia amethystina, 59, *59*, 66–67

Utricularia cornuta, 57, 60, *60*, 62, 66–67
Utricularia floridana, 60, *60*, *65*, 66–67
Utricularia foliosa, 61, *61*, 66–67
Utricularia gibba, *57*, *58*, 61, *61*, *65*, 66–67
Utricularia inflata, 61, *61*, 63, *65*, 66–67
Utricularia juncea, 60, 62, *62*, 66–67
Utricularia olivacea, 62, *62*, 66–67
Utricularia purpurea, 62, *62*, 63, *65*, 66–67
Utricularia radiata, 61, 63, *63*, 66–67
Utricularia resupinata, 63, *63*, 66–67
Utricularia simulans, 63, *63*, 66–67
Utricularia striata, 64, *64*, 66–67
Utricularia subulata, 64, *64*, 66–67

Vasconcelos, Reginaldo, 77
Veitch Nursery, 39
Venus flytrap, ix, 1, 4, *4*, 5, 6, 11, 17, 18, 24, 26, 27, 29, 31–38, *31*, *32*, *35*, *36*, *37*, 58, 86, 97

water, 1, 3, 5, 11, 13, 14, 15, 16, 18, 19, 21, *21*, 23, 24, 25, 28, 29, 30, 31, 35, 40, 49, 57, 58, 59, 60, 61, 62, 66–67, 69, 70, 71, 73, 77, 80, 85–88, 90, 93, 95, 96–97
water tray method, 1, 21, *21*, 27, 61, 96–97
white pitcher plant, 46.
    See also Sarracenia leucophylla
Willson, Minnie Moore, 16

yellow pitcher plant, 45.
    See also Sarracenia flava

About the Author

Learn Florida's carnivorous plant history and their care—presented by a vegetarian! Join national columnist and nurseryman **Kenny Coogan** as he shares the predatory qualities of these spectacular plants. Florida has more species of carnivorous plants than any other state in the United States. Understanding their unique niche in the ecosystem will help with their necessary conservation.

Coogan has a master's degree in global sustainability and is passionate about Florida's wildlife and plants. His professional experience with carnivorous plants started in 2011 when he cofounded the Western New York Carnivorous Plant club. He has published over 400 articles on pets, livestock, and gardening for publications including *Countryside, Hobby Farms, Chickens, Backyard Beekeeping, Backyard Poultry,* and *Florida Gardening* magazines. Coogan is an active member with the International Carnivorous Plant Society, serving as the Education Director. He currently runs a successful carnivorous plant nursery in Tampa, Florida.

For more details visit kennycoogan.com.

Also by Kenny Coogan:
A Tenrec Named Trey: (And other odd lettered animals that like to play)
99½ Homesteading Poems: A Backyard Guide to Raising Creatures, Growing Opportunity, and Cultivating Community